Teaching Students to Write

M000218341

▶ **Argument**
Essays That Define
Comparison/Contrast Essays
Personal Narratives
Research Reports
Fictional Narratives

The Dynamics of Writing Instruction series

Peter Smagorinsky
Larry R. Johannessen
Elizabeth A. Kahn
Thomas M. McCann

HEINEMANN
Portsmouth, NH

Heinemann
361 Hanover Street
Portsmouth, NH 03801–3912
www.heinemann.com

Offices and agents throughout the world

© 2011 by Peter Smagorinsky, Elizabeth A. Kahn, and Thomas M. McCann

The authors and publisher wish to thank those who have generously given permission to reprint borrowed material:

Figure 2–2: "Bewildered in Bettendorf" from *Explorations: Introductory Activities for Literature and Composition, 7–12,* by Peter Smagorinsky, Tom McCann, and Stephen Kern. Copyright © 1987 by the National Council of Teachers of English. Used with permission.

Library of Congress Cataloging-in-Publication Data
Teaching students to write argument / Peter Smagorinsky . . . [et al.].
    p. cm. – (The dynamics of writing instruction series)
  Includes bibliographical references.
  ISBN-13: 978-0-325-03400-3
  ISBN-10: 0-325-03400-1
    1. English language—Composition and exercises—Study and teaching (Middle school). 2. English language—Composition and exercises—Study and teaching (Secondary). 3. Persuasion (Rhetoric) —Study and teaching (Middle school). 4. Persuasion (Rhetoric)— Study and teaching (Secondary).   I. Smagorinsky, Peter.

LB1631.T3318 2011
808'.0420712—dc23   2011034009

Editor: Anita Gildea *and* Lisa Luedeke
Development editor: Alan Huisman
Production: Vicki Kasabian
Cover design: Monica Ann Crigler
Typesetter: Valerie Levy / Drawing Board Studios
Manufacturing: Steve Bernier

Printed in the United States of America on acid-free paper
15 14 13 12 PAH 3 4 5

CONTENTS

Preface   v

Why Teach Students to Write Arguments?   1

CHAPTER 1
Teaching a Model for Reasoning   5

CHAPTER 2
Teaching Students to Expand Their Arguments   27

CHAPTER 3
Considering Competing Points of View   44

CHAPTER 4
Constructing Gateways   59

CHAPTER 5
What Makes This a Structured Process Approach?   75

References   85

Preface

Despite all the attention that writing instruction received during the final decades of the twentieth century, the teaching of writing in middle and high schools remains, at best, uneven. National Writing Project sites have conducted countless summer institutes, and new books about teaching writing appear routinely in publishers' catalogues. Yet assessments continue to find that students' writing is less accomplished than teachers might hope. Undoubtedly, the assessments themselves are not what they ought to be (Hillocks 2002). But even those with relatively good reputations, such as the National Assessment of Educational Progress, find that students in the United States are not writing as well as many people expect them to. What's going on here? And will yet another book about teaching writing make a difference?

We have written this series of small books in the hope that they will provide alternatives for teachers who are dissatisfied with teaching five-paragraph themes, traditional grammar lessons, and other form-driven writing approaches. This book employs what we call *structured process*, an approach developed by George Hillocks during his years as a middle school English teacher in Euclid, Ohio, during the 1960s. Hillocks and his students have researched this method and found it highly effective (Hillocks, Kahn, and Johannessen 1983; Smith 1989; Smagorinsky 1991; Lee 1993). In a comprehensive research review, Hillocks (1986) found that over a twenty-year period, structured process writing instruction provided greater gains for student writers than did any other method of teaching writing.

We have spent a collective 120-plus years using structured process instruction in our high school English classes. We do not claim to have discovered the one best way to teach writing; rather, our goal is to explain in detail a method that we all found successful in our teaching. We hope you find this book useful and that your teaching benefits from reading and using the entire series.

How to Get the Most Out of This Book and This Series

The six books in this series help middle and high school teachers teach writing using a structured process approach, a method based on sound theory and research. Each book follows a similar format, focusing on a different type of writing: argument (the focus of this volume), personal narrative, fictional narrative, comparison/contrast essays, essays that define, and research reports. Although there are some general writing processes that apply to all types of writing, different kinds of writing require unique strategies. Therefore, the instructional activities in each book are tailored to that specific kind of writing.

The books show you how to design and orchestrate activities within an interactive and collaborative environment in which your students themselves experiment with ideas, debate these ideas with their peers, decide what and how to write, determine how to assess the quality of their writing, and discuss their work as a group. They include classroom-tested activities, detailed lesson sequences, and supporting handouts. The instruction is detailed enough to use as a daily lesson plan but general enough that you can modify it to accommodate your own curriculum and the specific needs of your students.

Most writing instruction emphasizes form. With a structured process approach, students first learn the thinking processes and strategies at the heart of a specific kind of writing, then consider form. This approach also recognizes that students write best when they want to communicate something that matters to them. The books show you how to introduce issues, dilemmas, and scenarios that capture students' interest and invoke the critical and creative thinking necessary to write powerfully and effectively. Samples of student writing are included; they illustrate students' learning and can also be used as instructional material for students to critique.

You may incorporate these books into a multiyear English language arts program, perhaps starting with personal narratives and fictional narratives in the earlier grades and moving to arguments, comparison/contrast essays, essays that define, and research reports in later grades. Alternatively, all six books in the series could constitute a yearlong writing course. Another option is to repeat modified sequences from one book at sequential grade levels, so students deal with that particular form at increasing degrees of complexity.

Although many of the activities and teaching strategies in these books can be used in isolation, they are most effective when included within a sequence of instruction in which students participate in increasingly challenging activities designed to help them become independent writers.

What's in This Book

A brief introduction explains our reasons for teaching students how to do the kind of thinking and writing required by argument. Chapters 1 through 4 show you *how* to teach students to write arguments using structured process instruction; in them we describe classroom teaching strategies, provide a sequence of activities and handouts, and show examples of student work. Chapter 5 explains the structured process approach to teaching writing and its two main tenets, *environmental teaching* and *inquiry instruction*. This will help you understand why we designed the instruction modeled in this book the way we did; it will also help you design your own units of instruction in the future.

Why Teach Students to Write Arguments?

In *Clueless in Academe*, Gerald Graff (2003) asserts that argument is at the heart of academic endeavor: "For American students to do better—all of them, not just twenty percent—they need to know that summarizing and making arguments is the name of the game in academia" (3). Graff insists that understanding the arguments of others and advancing one's own arguments are essential to what students do in school. He also believes schools downplay argument's preeminence. Perhaps that's because people think students cannot contend with the cognitive demands of argument until they reach the upper grades of high school (Crowhurst 1990, 1988) or feel that argument connotes combat and volatility.

Argument is not verbal combat used only during competitive debate. Argument is an element of discussion and deliberation, activities that suggest group inquiry and a combined effort to arrive at deeper understanding, stronger resolution, and better decisions. There may be times when an advocate hopes to win a point against an opponent, and there are few occasions when a prosecuting attorney acknowledges the merits of the defense attorney's arguments. But on many occasions recognizing and fairly assessing opposing views *does* strengthen understanding and is in itself persuasive.

Being able to write arguments proficiently is important to doing well in school (and on school and state assessments) and to developing critical thinking. Schools may begin to place more emphasis on argument now that the Common Core State Standards emphasize that students should be able to "write arguments to support claims in an analysis of substantive topics or texts, using valid reasoning and relevant and sufficient evidence." Similarly, the College

Readiness Standards offered by the College Board emphasize unity, organization, and coherence as key features of strong writing.

In schools, argument writing appears under all sorts of labels: report writing, persuasive writing, thesis writing, critical analysis, and so on. The terms *persuasion* and *argument* are often used interchangeably, as teachers, textbook writers, and test makers ask students to write arguments to persuade an audience about a critical question (Hillocks 2010).

Our own research (McCann 1989, for example) convinces us that middle and high school students are aware of the basic demands of argument and use this knowledge to anticipate challenges from their parents and teachers. At the same time, many adolescents struggle when writing arguments. And teaching them the technical aspects of syllogistic logic doesn't help much. Exercises in logic and lessons on technical terms don't seem to help even college students prepare better written arguments (Karbach 1987; Kneupper 1978).

However, Michael Smith (1984) notes that by responding to the questions *why? so what?* and *who says?* every day, learners begin to recognize and satisfy the requirements of argument. Through a careful sequence of interactive experiences beginning with oral conversations, you can help your students learn to compose logically elaborated argumentation essays.

While this book treats argument as a specific genre, the logical thinking at its core is necessary for many kinds of writing, particularly essays that define (in which the writer supports criterion statements with relevant examples) and comparison/contrast essays (in which the writer supports claims about the objects or ideas she or he is discussing). It is also an effective way to approach research reports (see that volume of this series).

Argumentation also supports students' understanding of what they read. A prereading argument activity focused on conflicts that parallel or otherwise relate to the conflicts of literary characters lets students understand what the characters face and feel. Students can also assess a broad theme in a novel or nonfiction book they are about to read.

We hope the activities in this book will also help students develop habits of thinking that will serve them well as citizens in their communities. In a narrow sense, they may want to write letters to legislators, newspaper editors, or the local school board. More broadly, deliberation about local issues that includes fair attention to and assessment of many different perspectives encourages a sense of community; the decisions and actions of others affect everyone, and the good of the community is promoted by civil, rational discourse, not by getting one's way at all costs (O'Donnell-Allen 2011).

Chapters 1, 2, and 3 show you how to teach students to write arguments, beginning with relatively simple problems and relatively modest products and moving on to more elaborate ones. Chapter 4 suggests ways for you to construct your own inquiry-based activities to help students write arguments and provides two examples. The writing the students produce in any and all of these lessons also introduces them to themes they will encounter in their study of literature.

The activities in each chapter are inquiry-based. Students, in groups, explore possible solutions to a specific, concrete, familiar problem. There is a specific audience to address, a central purpose for writing, a body of information to be examined, and a framework for completing the analysis. Students can solve the problem in a variety of ways given their overall purpose and any specified constraints. Because they are using specific strategies in a particular context, they are not arguing a position for the sake of arguing but rather to accomplish a goal. They will usually have a lot to say. Ideally, while thinking and talking with their peers, they develop procedures they can use independently in other situations, with other information.

By deliberately working through several stages on the way to completing a piece of writing, students have an opportunity to construct an argument that both matters to them and influences others. They address a particular problem using specific problem-solving strategies and rehearse their ideas by discussing them with other students before they put them on paper. Producing the argument helps them understand some common critical questions more deeply.

Teaching a Model for Reasoning

The sequence of instruction in this book teaches students to present their thinking by way of claims, grounds (data, examples, evidence), warrants, backing, rebuttals, and responses (Toulmin 1958; Toulmin et al. 1984). To produce a strong argument writers need to think and write about a problem in connection with a related body of information and communicate their opinions to a specific audience honestly and convincingly, not simply follow a generic template. But even students as young as fourth graders can learn to construct reasonable arguments (McCann 1989).

Stage 1. Introducing the Argumentation Sequence

Middle school students need help linking units of thought in a coherent and organized way. This lesson, for fifth graders (but appropriate at later grades), has the following goals (which will also be your evaluation criteria):

- Teach students to examine information and draw logical conclusions about trends and patterns.

- Teach students to write a coherent, logical paragraph that expresses a claim, supports the claim by citing relevant data, and interprets the data.

Three questions influenced its design: *What kind of problem will the students care about? What kind of data will support their thinking about the problem? What activities will trigger students' thinking and purposeful interaction?*

You'll use these materials:

- Plain yellow three-inch-square sticky notes

- Florescent three-inch-square sticky notes

- Eighteen-by-twenty-four-inch chart paper, each sheet labeled with a category: Music/Dance, Shopping, Sports, Socializing, Time with Family, TV/Movies, Computers and Video Games, Reading, and Gardening Social media

EPISODE 1.1. Tell students: "I want to get to know all of you as quickly as possible. I don't have time to go around the room and interview everyone, so I've come up with a way to get a sense of who you are. I especially want to know about the activities you find the most fun or engrossing." Model by sharing some of your own interests, distinguishing activities that are pleasant and nice from those that are totally engrossing. For example, you might say that watching the news on television or walking your dog are pleasant activities, but reading a good book, playing tennis, or talking to an old friend on the phone are totally engrossing.

EPISODE 1.2. Distribute the sticky note pads and give these directions:

1. On the plain yellow stickies, briefly jot down activities that interest you, one per note.

2. On the brightly colored stickies, jot down activities in which you become so involved you lose track of time.

Data

The information on these sticky notes becomes the data set.

EPISODE 1.3. Have students, in groups, talk for about ten minutes about the things they like to do. This informal talk will trigger ideas to write on the sticky notes. Give students time to write their activities on the sticky notes, one activity per note.

EPISODE 1.4. (about fifteen minutes) Ask students to organize their sticky notes into the category headings displayed on the sheets of chart paper posted around the room: Music/Dance, Shopping, Sports, Socializing, Time with Family, TV/Movies, Computers and Video Games, Reading, and Gardening. Then have a few students at a time affix their notes to the appropriate sheets of chart paper, as shown in the photo in Figure 1–1.

Figure 1–1. Collecting, Categorizing, and Comparing Data

EPISODE 1.5. Ask students what these charts tell them about what fifth graders especially enjoy doing. Tell them to think beyond what they *personally* enjoy and draw their conclusions from the patterns they see on the chart paper. Here's a sample discussion:

You: Based on what you see on the chart paper, what would you say the students in this class especially like to do?

Bethany: We really like sports.

You: Why would you say that?

Bethany: Look at all of the sticky notes.

You: What do you mean?

Bethany: There are a lot of sticky notes on the sheet that says *sports*.

You: So what?

Draw conclusion about the class in general.

Carson: There are probably more there than anywhere else.

You: So you would say that sports is the highest-ranking choice?

Carson: That's right.

You: Then what would you say this class is far less interested in doing?

Katrina: We don't really like gardening.

You: How do you know?

Katrina: There are only four stickies there.

You: So what does that mean?

Katrina: If it was popular, there would be a lot of notes.

With the students' help, count the number of sticky notes under each category and the total number of sticky notes to provide further information on which students can base their judgment.

You: How do you know the students in this class especially like sports?

Araceli: Look at all of the sticky notes.

You: What do you mean?

Araceli: There are like a million notes under *sports*.

You: A million? How many, exactly?

Freddy: There were 88 votes.

You: Since there were 400 total votes, that comes to 22 percent. What does that show?

Stephania: That 22 percent of our class likes sports.

You: Is that true? Let's see. How many of you like sports? [All hands will probably go up.] Look at that. Everyone likes sports: that's 100 percent. So you can't say that only 22 percent of the class likes sports. What does that number mean?

Freddy: That 22 percent of all the votes were for sports.

You: That sounds more accurate—that 22 percent of all of our notes went on the big sheet of paper labeled *sports*. But that doesn't sound like a lot.

Colleen: Yeah, but compared with gardening or reading, it really is a lot.

You: So you are saying that while the 22 percent might seem small, it is really the largest percentage of our votes. Is that right?

Colleen: You got it.

By guiding students' thinking like this you help them look beneath the surface of their initial impressions and use the organization of the data to sharpen the conclusions they draw.

EPISODE 1.6. Help the students move from generating and analyzing data to writing about their interpretation. Ask them to write a paragraph that states a conclusion and supports the conclusion with the relevant information. Thinking out loud, compose a sample paragraph about your fellow teachers' plans for the weekend. For example, you might say:

> Yesterday I asked all the teachers at our school what their plans were for the weekend. I discovered that many of them like gardening. You might wonder how I figured this out. Here is how I know. They talked about a lot of plans, but sixteen of the twenty-six teachers said that they planned to do some gardening. That's more than half. You might say, "So what?" The next most popular activity was shopping, with ten of the twenty-six teachers saying that they planned to shop over the weekend. I have to conclude that gardening is a very popular activity among teachers at our school, because more than half of the teachers chose to garden over the weekend. The teachers chose gardening more often than any other activity.

You might write the following paragraph:

> When I asked the teachers at our school about their plans for the weekend, sixteen of the twenty-six teachers said that they planned to do some gardening. The next most popular activity was shopping. Ten of the twenty-six teachers said that they planned to shop over the weekend. I conclude that gardening is a very popular activity among teachers at our school, because more than half of the teachers chose to garden over the weekend. The teachers chose gardening more often than any other activity.

Your goal is to model a *process* for converting raw information to analyzed data to a written opinion based on the data.

EPISODE 1.7. Ask each student to write a draft paragraph, while you monitor their attempts and help as needed. Below are examples of the kinds of paragraphs students may produce:

> Out of all the fifth graders in our class, they liked sports the best. The survey we did showed that 88 out of 400 votes were for sports. That may not seem like much, but gardening only got 2 votes. The other categories got around 12 to 53 votes. Compared to the others, 88 votes for sports looks much bigger.
>
> *Emily*

> The fifth-grade students in our class like to play sports. In a recent survey, 22 percent of the total votes was for sports. That's high because the ones that have fewer that 88 votes in the survey will be lower than 22 percent. All of the other ones are less than 88 votes. This result shows that fifth-grade kids like to play sports.
>
> *Blanca*

> The students in our class really like to play sports. In a recent survey, 88 votes were for sport, out of 400 total. This is a lot more than other categories, which many of them only got 20 or lower votes. The result of this survey showed that the majority of the fifth graders enjoy playing sports.
>
> *Kaeli*

> The students in our fifth grade class really like sport and social activities. Some popular sports are baseball, softball, and soccer. Some popular socializing is playing with friends. I know all of this from a recent survey with Post-it notes. There were 88 entries for sports and 53 entries for socializing. This survey shows the top two popular entries answered by real kids. So there is proof that out of 400 entries, 53 of them were for socializing and 88 of them were for sports.
>
> *Mary*

EPISODE 1.8. Call on volunteers to read their paragraphs aloud. After listening to each example, comment on (or ask students to comment on) the degree to which the paragraph followed the model for reasoning:

- The writer made a claim.

- The writer supported the claim by citing data.

- The writer explained the meaning or significance of the data.

EPISODE 1.9. Have students, in pairs, exchange paragraphs and spend about ten minutes editing them. They should:

1. Check whether the writer made a claim, supported it with data, and explained the meaning of the data.

2. Judge whether or not the writer's reasoning was logical.

3. Check spelling, punctuation, capitalization, and complete sentences.

preview

explain

logical

rubric ?

EPISODE 1.10. Have students hand in the final version of their paragraph.

Stage 2. Arguing in Favor of a Choice

In the previous activity, it was obvious which activity was most popular. Students could look at the charts and see immediately which category got the most votes. It was easy to assume that any reasonable reader would draw the same conclusion. But evidence is not always self-explanatory: indeed, in this case the students confused the percentage of votes cast for sports with the percentage of students who liked sports. Students need rules for interpreting data, and the rules can change from context to context.

This activity helps students devise the rules they will rely on to interpret the significance of certain features or attributes in a visual data set. Here are your goals for this series of lessons:

- All students will develop a model for informal reasoning.

✓ • All students, using a model for informal reasoning, will analyze data and draw logical conclusions.

✓ • All students, using a model for informal reasoning, will apply
criteria to judge the relative merits of a set of proposed school
mascots and prepare a written analysis. *or motto?*
Whatever it takes to graduate,

Hmm?

EPISODE 2.1.   Introduce the activity by noting that mascots are a
way to identify and distinguish a school or a community. Students,
staff, and graduates frequently take pride in the school mascot. Ask
students to share their impressions, feelings, and associations about
their own school mascot. You could use these questions as prompts:

- What is the mascot?

- How was the mascot selected?

- Do you like the mascot? Why?

- If you were to select a different mascot, what would it be?
Why would you select it?

EPISODE 2.2.   Display the four mascots in Figure 1–2 on a projector.
Ask students to evaluate the merits of each:

- Do you think the mascot is a good one?

- If you like it, what makes it a good mascot?

- If you don't like it, what makes it a bad mascot?

Initially, your students will probably dismiss the mascots as "stu-
pid" or "dumb." Ask them to explain. For example, a student might
observe that a pretzel isn't something she would take pride in and
wouldn't be a good representative of the school at competitive
sports events because it isn't fierce.

EPISODE 2.3.   Divide the class into groups of three or four. Ask each
group to propose four or five rules a new school could use to select a
mascot. As the students talk, go from group to group, checking their
progress and paraphrasing some of their ideas. Here's an example of
how a group discussion might go:

Figure 1–2. Examples of School Mascots

**Pretzel
Freeport, Illinois**

**Banana Slug, University of
California Santa Cruz**

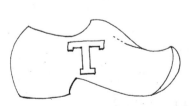

**Wooden Shoe
Teutopolis, Illinois**

**Alice
Vincennes, Indiana**

Jacqui: What about big?

Mary Jane: Maybe could be funny, like slugs?

Carl: Sure!

Mary Jane: Needs to be unusual; stands out.

Jimmy: Interesting.

Carl: It could also be unique.

Mary Jane: Well, that's the same as stands out.

Jacqui: Maybe stands out is too hard.

Jimmy: Intimidating.

Carl: Yea, that's a good one.

Jimmy: Proud.

Mary Jane: Has to have something to do with the school.

Carl: Representing it!

Jacqui: Large instead of tiny.

Mary Jane: No! Think about the slugs. They aren't big.

Jacqui: Think about the Dukes [the mascot for a nearby high school].

Carl: We all like the Dukes!

Jacqui: Strong. We like that!

Jimmy: Powerful.

Mary Ann: That's like strong.

Jacqui: What's our school color?

Jimmy: Blue and gray.

Jacqui: Okay, has something to do with the color.

EPISODE 2.4. Call on representatives from each group to report their "rules." Prompt the students to paraphrase, clarify, and evaluate the suggestions in order to determine a common set of criteria for judging a good mascot. Record these criteria on an overhead transparency or a white board and ask all the students to copy the final version. Here are some possibilities:

- Mascots are often strong or tough or fierce animals (Detroit Lions, University of Kentucky Wildcats, University of Wisconsin Badgers).

- Mascots often have some connection to the school, community, or state, especially when the name is unique (Joliet Ironmen, Purdue Boilermakers, Wyoming Cowboys, Green Bay Packers, Cobden Appleknockers, Nebraska Cornhuskers, Savannah Sandgnats, Oklahoma Sooners).

- Mascots should be something that someone would be proud to be (University of Washington Huskies, James Madison University Dukes, Milwaukee Admirals, Kenyon College Lords), although some choices are puzzling in this regard (Texas Christian University Horned Frogs).

- The mascot should be appropriate for both boys and girls.

- The mascot should be something that community members and students can relate to.

- Mascots usually have names that fit well (sound good) with the school name, often using alliteration or assonance (e.g., Elmhurst Eagles, Leo Lions, Richmond Raiders; not Elmhurst Wagon Wheels, or Leo Crested Cockatoos).

- Mascots can be funny or rely on puns, as in the Macon Whoopee (minor league hockey team), the Poca Dot (West Virginia high school), the Gwinnett Gwizzly (minor league basketball team), and the Polo Marco (Illinois high school).

- Although mascots in the past often took names or descriptions of Native Americans, today such names are often viewed as controversial and are avoided (Wynnewood Savages, Cleveland Indians, Illinois Fighting Illini).

EPISODE 2.5. Ask your students to imagine that the John L. Lewis Elementary School has just opened but has not yet selected a mascot. Hand out the assignment in Figure 1–3 and the mascots shown in Figure 1–4.

Figure 1–3. Mascot Problem

The John L. Lewis Elementary School is having a contest to select the school mascot. The mascot's image will appear on the gym floor, on school stationery, on school-spirit clothing, and on school publications. Four drawings (attached) have been selected for final consideration, and you are one of the judges. Here is what you need to do:

Evaluate each of the drawings, and write an explanation of why it would or would not be a good mascot, based on the evaluation criteria that the class developed together.

Keep the evaluation criteria in mind, remember the profile of the school and community, and study the details and attributes of the proposed mascots.

Profile of John L. Lewis Elementary School

John L. Lewis Elementary School opened two years ago in Floodrock, Illinois. Floodrock is located in Saline County, which is in the very southern region of the state. The current enrollment at John L. Lewis is 315 students.

The surrounding area has two major industries: farming and coal mining. The area has long been rich in coal mines, and many families in Saline County have had some connection to the coal mines. Since fewer homes and businesses depend on coal as an energy source these days, the activities in the mines have slowed and the coal companies employ few residents. Nevertheless, the citizens of Floodrock and the rest of Saline County still associate themselves with the coal industry. The school is named after John L. Lewis, who was the president of the United Mine Workers of America for 40 years.

Figure 1–4. Proposed Mascots for John L. Lewis Elementary School

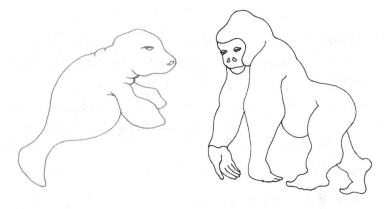

Manatee

Lowland Gorilla

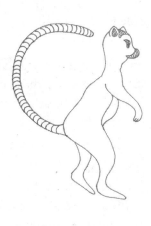

Lemur

Miner

EPISODE 2.6. Lead a discussion in which students identify the attributes associated with each mascot: *What features or attributes do you associate with a gorilla? What features or attributes do you associate with a manatee? How do these attributes match the criteria the class expressed for selecting a good mascot?* For example:

Nicholas: Manatees are kind of slow moving. Some people call them sea cows. No one would want to think of himself as a sea cow.

Barbara: Gorillas are really strong. That would be good if you want to frighten the other teams. But gorillas have nothing to do with Illinois.

Nancy: And it doesn't sound right—the Lewis Gorillas.

You: So what if it doesn't sound good?

Nancy: You want a mascot name that sounds right for the school. Then the cheers would sound right.

You: How about the lemurs?

Ed: That sounds better—the Lewis Lemurs—but who would want to be a lemur? They are like shy little animals. The mascot has to be strong or powerful so that people want to be like it.

EPISODE 2.7. Tell the class you expect each student to write a *thorough* and *logical* paragraph about one of the proposed mascots. Then demonstrate what a writer might think while composing one. In the following example, the thoughts you would say aloud are in brackets:

The Bobcat is a good example of a mascot for Gotha School. [*Why would I say that?*] A bobcat is a very smart animal and is a strong defender of its home and family. [*Why is this important?*] A student at Gotha can take pride in being represented by an animal that is a smart and strong protector of its family. [*But isn't a bobcat kind of a scary animal?*] Although the bobcat can be an aggressive fighter, it attacks to survive and to protect its young, and not to be mean.

Now ask the students to write their own paragraphs justifying the mascot they chose for Lewis Elementary School. Here are two typical student examples:

> The miners are a good mascot for John L. Lewis elementary school. Everyone in the school can take pride in their past because their town was a mining town. Another thing, miners have to be strong to get whatever they are mining. These characteristics are important because kids should be proud about their mascot, and their past.
>
> *Hannah,* Grade 5

> The Lowland Gorilla is a good mascot for John L. Lewis school. A Lowland Gorilla is very intimidating, very smart, and is very strong and powerful. The Lowland Gorilla can make the students at John L. Lewis proud. All mascots should be strong and powerful so that the student can be proud and take pride in it.
>
> *Kristian,* Grade 5

Stage 3. Applying the Procedures to a More Complex Problem

Students are now ready to consider a more complicated problem relying on a similar data set but requiring more extensive analysis and explanation. In this activity students think about how to find appropriate homes for dogs available for adoption. In both small-group and large-group discussions, students grapple with matching dogs and prospective owners. Defending decisions that are questioned and challenged by their classmates, they do the same kind of thinking that later guides their writing when they turn their notes into written arguments.

EPISODE 3.1.   Introduce the problem by handing out and discussing Figure 1–5, which is a summary of the pet adoption process followed by a description of a typical rescue center.

Figure 1–5. Pet Adoption Process

Every day, Monday through Saturday, visitors come to the Floodrock Pet Rescue Center, in Floodrock, Illinois, hoping to adopt a pet. The workers at the rescue center care very much for the animals they protect and want to place them in good homes, with loving and responsible pet owners. Since they can't let people just walk in and pick out any pet that they want, they have worked out the following process for dog adoption:

1. Each dog is categorized by its particular characteristics: big or small, companion or worker, leisurely or active, social or shy, and so forth.

2. Each person who wants to adopt a dog must fill out an application. The answers to the application questions help the rescue center workers know what kind of dog would be a good match for that person.

3. The rescue center manager reviews the dogs' profiles and the applications, meets with the people who want to adopt a pet, and recommends the best match. For example, a person who has a small apartment and spends most leisure time reading or watching television is not the best person to own a big dog that wants to exercise, run in open spaces, and meet other dogs and people.

EPISODE 3.2.   To help students understand what pet rescue center workers do, let them experience the process.

1. First have each student fill out a preadoption application form (you can find sample forms on animal shelter websites).

2. Hold up a picture of a mature boxer and tell the students about the dog: "Lady is a two-year-old boxer. She has lived in an apartment in the city with a young professional who had to leave the dog alone for long periods of time. Lady has not often been around people or other dogs, so she

is rather shy. She loves to exercise but also enjoys quiet companionship. Lady weighs sixty pounds." Let students discuss how Lady would fit into their own households.

Figure 1–6. Instructions for the Pet Adoption Activity

Your Job as a Team: This week there is a new group of applicants who want to adopt dogs, and there is a new bunch of dogs that are eligible for adoption.

1. Working with your partners, categorize the dogs ("couch potato," "busy bee," "free spirit," etc.) and then describe the characteristics of the best home and the most appropriate owner for each dog.

2. Study each application submitted by someone who wants to adopt a dog. Judge whether the person is suited to owning a dog and the best type of dog for that person. Discuss your decisions with your partners and explain why you made the matches you did.

3. During the discussion, take notes in complete sentences. Describe each person who has applied to adopt a dog. State the match and explain why the match is a good one. If someone is not an appropriate match for any dog, explain why.

4. Explain to the whole class the matches you recommend and why you recommend them. Other students may have questions about your choices, so you'll want to be prepared to respond.

The Materials:

1. Pictures and descriptions of six dogs currently available for adoption.

2. Applications/profiles of four possible dog owners.

(continues)

Figure 1–6. Instructions for the Pet Adoption Activity (*continued*)

Write About Your Matches: After you have discussed the possible matches thoroughly and have taken notes, write your own individual letter to Ms. Kay Neins, the Manager of Floodrock Pet Rescue Center. Ms. Neins is just returning from a long vacation and will have to counsel the people who want to adopt a dog. Because she's been away she's unfamiliar with the new dogs and the new applicants. Write a letter to Ms. Neins to prepare her for her meetings with hopeful owners: explain the judgments you made as you matched persons with pets. Use the following steps to guide you:

Step 1. Using your notes, compose a draft letter. You needn't bother with a personal introduction, but do let Ms. Neins know that you are aware of the challenge she faces in matching potential pet owners with the right dogs. The introduction will preview the paragraphs contained in the bulk of the letter. Also include a conclusion in which you review your judgments about matching persons with dogs. In short, your letter will have an introduction (noting the current problem), a paragraph about each potential dog owner and the appropriate dog, and a conclusion that generally reviews how to match people with dogs.

Step 2. In class, exchange your draft with a classmate. Allow your classmate to ask you questions for clarification. Your reviewer may want to see that you applied the rescue center's guidelines for matching pets with owners or may want to know more about the dogs or the people interested in being dog owners. This is a clue that you may need to provide more detailed descriptions or explanations. Remember that Ms. Nein will not have all the preadoption applications and the dogs in front of her when she reads the letter. She will need your descriptions to help her recall the details of each. Also, rely on your classmate and any available adult reader to help you with spelling, sentence and paragraph formation, and punctuation.

Step 3. Rewrite your letter, incorporating any necessary changes. Your letter should be neat and error-free.

EPISODE 3.3 Divide class into small groups and give each group a copy of the instructions in Figure 1–6, along with a folder containing descriptions of six dogs up for adoption and four completed applications.

An example of a student response is shown in Figure 1–7. In her letter, Olivia states the problem and explains why it is significant. She recommends her matches systematically, stating the attributes of the dogs and the characteristics of the potential owner and the owner's environment. She also explains how she connected various details to reach her conclusions. A response like this is developed through reasoned thought as prompted by the activity:

1. Before the students discuss the potential adoptions in small groups, they become familiar with the adoption decision-making process under your guidance.

2. They work with accessible data.

3. Disagreements within the group force students to explain recommended matches.

4. They take written notes about their decisions and the reasons for those decisions.

5. While writing their argument they receive feedback from their classmates and from you.

Figure 1–7. Olivia's Letter to Ms. Neins

March 15

Dear Ms. Kay Neine,

I understand that you are struggling with pairing dogs with the right owners. For the sake of the pet and the owner, it is important to match the right dog with the most appropriate owner. I am writing to you to help you find homes for the dogs. I think some great pairs are the following: Emily Adamo and Bailey, Mike Lillis and Rascal, Mr. Smithers and Wolfie, and Vivian Glaussen and Shep.

(continues)

Figure 1–7. Olivia's Letter to Ms. Neins (*continued*)

I think that Bailey is a good dog for Emily Adamo. Bailey is a Golden Retriever. She is a good dog for Emily because Emily runs daily and Bailey is a running dog and can run with Emily every day. Emily works as a child psychologist and has three children of her own. She works in her home office from late in the afternoon into early evening hours. When she is at work she has a husband and three kids to watch over Bailey, who loves the company of humans. Bailey has a reputation for being good with children, so she will be a safe dog for Emily's children and for the young visitors to the home.

Rascal is probably a good dog for Mike Lillis because he lives and works on a farm. He wants a dog that can help him work on the farm and Rascal is a work dog. Rascal is a Dalmatian and dogs of that breed like to run. Mike works long hours and Rascal will be in the barn. There is no fence around Mike's yard but also there are not a lot of cars so he will not go running off into the streets. Rascal is a willing worker, but needs to be trained. Mike is an experienced farmer so he will be able to train him.

I think Wolfie is a good dog for Mr. Smithers. Wolfie is an Akita/Huskie mix. He is a good dog for Mr. Smithers because he wants a guard dog and Wolfie is a guard dog. When Mr. Smithers is gone for nine hours, Wolfie will be able to stay home and be okay, because Wolfie is not very active because he is getting old. When Mr. Smithers is out for long hours, he will need a guard dog to watch over the house. Wolfie can do this job! While Mr. Smithers and his wife are not home, Wolfie will stay in the laundry room and the room is rather large so he will have room to walk and play around. In the winter when the Smithers are gone, the room is heated so Wolfie will stay warm. They have a fenced-in yard with a chain-link fence about four feet high, so this gives him enough room to run around and play in a protected area. I think these two would be great companions.

(*continues*)

Figure 1–7. Olivia's Letter to Ms. Neins (*continued*)

I think a good dog for Vivian Glaussen is Shep, a mixed breed. It's a good dog for her because she is an older woman and does not need an active dog bouncing off the walls. She lives in a small condominium so he won't have that much place to run around. However, Vivian does not have a yard, so she will take Shep to a nearby park. She does not work out of her home, but while Ms. Glaussen volunteers and visits friends, Shep will be home alone for approximately twelve hours per week, or approximately two hours per day. Shep is cautious around children, but that is okay because Vivian does not have children.

Thank you for taking the time and reading my letter. I am glad that I had a chance to recommend how to pair these dogs with the right owners. I hope you approve of my choices because the suggestions should lead to strong long-term relationships between dogs and owners.

Respectfully,
Olivia

Extensions

1. Have students apply these procedures to new problems that require data analysis and persuasion. In science class they can argue for the best diet for animals in the class-room terrarium, argue to prevent the conditions that result in water pollution, and so on. In history class they can argue the merits of different forms of government, the qualities of people running for elective office, and other aspects of civic participation. In language arts class they can argue which authors write the most interesting stories, which literary characters are responsible for which consequences, and so forth. In health class they can argue the consequences of diet, environmental exposure, and human or animal contact.

2. Have students conduct debates or mock trials on these and similar issues.

3. Have students write letters to city administrators or local media or express and defend their opinions on a personal blog. By extending their argumentation beyond the classroom, students see that the genre is not static but responds to the particular expectations and conventions that govern appropriate and effective communication within different communities.

Teaching Students to Expand
Their Arguments

These lessons address the broader planning necessary to connect a series of arguments to persuade the reader to take a specific action to eliminate or ameliorate a problem related to policy: arguments an observer might witness in a legislative body, like Congress or a city council, or read in the opinion and editorial pages of the newspaper. While the participants in the debate may agree that there is a problem and agree on the magnitude of the problem, they disagree about the action to take to make conditions better. For example, we might agree that the United States depends too heavily on foreign sources for energy; but we could disagree, perhaps vehemently, on how to reduce our dependence. We might see together that medical costs have escalated at an alarming rate and that far too many citizens live, precariously, without health insurance; yet we could disagree about how to accomplish health care reform. While legislators care deeply about these grave policy issues that call for action, adolescents fret about policy that governs parking at their school or that might eliminate snack cakes and deep fried foods from the school cafeteria. While the gravity of the problems may seem radically different, arguments to persuade others to take action in a particular direction use similar rhetorical means.

One model for these debatable policy questions is the *stock issues* approach. In the simplest form, one considers the need for change and proposes a solution that will eliminate or significantly reduce the negatives that define the need, after first considering the central policy question and all related problems. A call for action that would change the status quo triggers the debate. In some ways, this is a courtroom model: we assume the status quo is just fine—innocent, in a way—unless someone proves otherwise. The burden of proof is on the person who argues to change the current situation—or prosecutes the status quo.

Suppose a citizen asks that stop signs be installed at a specific intersection in the community. The public works manager and the local fiscal officer may resist the appeal—the change requires expenditures to buy the signs and put a crew to work installing them. The new signs will also disrupt current traffic patterns—motorists who previously passed unimpeded through the intersection now have to stop before proceeding cautiously. The town managers would be responsible for asking why the stop signs are needed.

Here's one defense, but one that probably wouldn't be successful: "I have been passing that intersection for years now, and all I see in the area is the green grass from the park and from the lawns on the other corners. A red sign there would be a striking complement to the dominant green, especially a sign in the shape of an octagon, which I consider the most beautiful of all geometric shapes."

An effective call for action shows that there are problems significant enough to warrant the change, even if that change causes inconvenience and costs money. In this case, a concerned citizen might claim that the intersection is dangerous, prompting the questions, *How do you know it's dangerous? How dangerous is it?* In other words, what makes the danger so *significant* or compelling that we would be willing to incur the trouble and expense of installing signs? Someone else might recall that during the last year there have been fourteen collisions at the intersection, one in which someone died and others in which occupants required hospitalization. One motorist drove into the park, where she severely damaged a water fountain and a bench. The problem now seems more serious.

Significance is of course a relative concept; we need to measure the seriousness of the *harms* (death and suffering or financial loss) against the degree of disruption and expense the change would cause. Most people would find the money needed to install four stop signs in order to prevent one human death and the suffering of others a worthwhile expenditure. However, when the change to the status quo means a significant expenditure or a diminution of liberty, a decision maker might hesitate, thinking, *It all depends*.

To pursue the stop sign question a little further, consider two more issues, ones that debaters would refer to as *inherency* and *solvency*. While town managers might admit to the seriousness of the loss of life, the human suffering, and the financial loss associated with the troublesome intersection, they might wonder whether it might be possible to eliminate the harms or reduce them significantly through some means that will cost little and still allow the free flow of traffic on the affected streets. Perhaps the local police just need to clamp down on speeding motorists, which would *generate* revenue. Maybe they could appeal to motorists to approach the intersection more cautiously in a brief message slipped in with the monthly water and sewer bill. The managers are thinking about possible *minor repairs* to the current system, repairs that would avoid a significant change. The citizen who petitioned for the stop signs would then consider the merits of this rebuttal position.

In their thorough analysis of the situation, the town managers have to weigh the potential benefits of correcting the problem against the costs of proposed solutions—perform a *cost-benefits* analysis. Are the problems inherent or can they be fixed without radical change? How workable is the stop sign solution? Will it bust our budget? Is it enforceable? Will it produce the desired effect without causing even greater problems?

The activities in this chapter require similar thinking processes of students and can be connected to literature or content study.

Stage 1. Introducing Extended Argument

This activity can be used on its own, to introduce a unit of study focused on an overarching question like *What is justice?* or in connection with Steinbeck's *Of Mice and Men*. (In the novel, the men who share the bunkhouse urge Candy to put his dog to sleep, arguing that in the long run Candy is not being kind to the dog by keeping it alive—an episode that prepares the reader to think about George's justification for shooting Lennie.)

EPISODE 1.1. Hand out and discuss Figure 2–1, Procedures for an Argument Case Analysis

EPISODE 1.2. Hand out the assignment in Figure 2–2.[1] Tell students that a young person has written a letter to an advice columnist about putting the family's old dog, Buster, to sleep and that you are going to use this letter to help them learn to think about critical issues and write mature arguments related to them. Ask them to read the assignment and then complete the argument planning sheet in Figure 2–3.

Figure 2–1. Procedures for an Argument Case Analysis

Define the Problem

What is the situation that you and other reasonable people are concerned about? What do you recommend (i.e., develop a new policy, or continue the current policy)? State explicitly what action should be taken.

Evaluate the Need

In order to persuade someone to take action, you need to show that there are compelling problems that need to be corrected.

• What are the *problems*? Consider one at a time.

• What *evidence* shows that there is a problem?

• How do you know that the problem is a *significant* one? What is the *impact*? Are lives lost? Are people hurt? Is there a significant financial loss?

If you think there is *no problem*, show how the *evidence* demonstrates that there is no problem or that the problem is insignificant.

(continues)

---

[1] An earlier version of this activity appeared in Smagorinsky, McCann, and Kern (1987).

Figure 2–1. Procedures for an Argument Case Analysis (*continued*)

Identify and Evaluate Opposing Judgments

Assume that there are reasonable persons who do not agree with you. What do they have to say? If you disagree, how do you judge that their testimonies or thinking fails or falls short? How can you present an opponent's position respectfully, without misrepresenting or ridiculing?

If we grant that there are problems, what is being done *now* to reduce or eliminate the problems? Is there reason to believe that someone is already doing all that can be done? Is there reason to believe that others have taken the best action to reduce the problems? If the current practices are lacking, what is wrong with them? Can we make a few minor changes without overhauling the current system?

Your Plan

What is *your plan* for improving matters? What makes you think that your plan will work? Is there reason to believe that your recommended plan of action will gain the desired effect (i.e., it is *efficacious*)? To what extent is there danger that your plan could cause more harm than good?

EPISODE 1.3. Students learn to write well in part by talking about the substance of their writing. Discussion, whether in small groups or as a whole class, reveals that thinkers in any one classroom approach the same problem in different ways. Perspectives collide; students encounter alternative ways of thinking about the problem and have to defend their positions. Lead a class discussion about how to respond to the boy's letter. Here is the kind of exchange that might take place:

You: Tell me about one problem that Buster faces.

Renee: He smells bad.

You: So what? I might know a lot of people who smell bad, and I'm not going to eliminate them. What's the big deal?

Figure 2–2. The Advice Columnist Assignment

You write an advice column, "Answerline," for a daily news-paper. Today you received the following letter. How can you respond in a way that offers the writer a feasible solution while remaining sensitive to the writer's feelings?

Dear Answerline:

I am thirteen years old. I have a dog named Buster, who is also thirteen. Buster is a boxer with a brown coat and a big patch of white fur across his broad chest. He used to be a very handsome dog. Now that he is very old he looks a little shabby.

I've had Buster for as long as I can remember. He and I used to do everything together. Buster used to meet me at school when class was dismissed. He even met me when it was cold and snowing. He stood outside the school door, snow piling on his shoulders. When I rode my bicycle, Buster ran beside me. When I went fishing, Buster romped in the shallow water, trying to catch the little sunfish. He's not very active any more, but he's still a good companion.

My family says it's time to have Buster put to sleep. They point out that he is very old and decrepit. My two older sisters complain that he smells bad, and he stinks up the whole house. They say that the house now smells so bad from his stench that they are too embarrassed to bring any friends home. Mom is also worried that the smell will get into the furniture, rugs, and curtains, and it will be very costly to clean or replace them. My mom says that since poor Buster has lost most of his teeth, it is very difficult to find things that he can eat; and he is not getting his proper nutrition. Buster is deaf and nearly blind. It took a long time to discover that Buster was blind because he knew how the furniture was arranged and he never bumped into anything. One day when I thought Buster was looking right at me, I tossed a frisbee to him. It hit him right between the eyes. He looked startled, like he didn't know what hit him. My dad says that he thinks Buster has arthritis, and it is very painful for him to move around.

(continues)

Figure 2–2. The Advice Columnist Assignment (*continued*)

I still think that I can take care of Buster. I've told my family that I'm willing to shampoo Buster every day and spray him with deodorant. I'll get up early each morning to prepare special soft foods for him. I would also watch Buster whenever I was home to make sure that he doesn't hurt himself.

My dad says that Buster would be better off dead because he is suffering and is no good to himself. But I don't know; I still love Buster and want to be with him. What should I do?

Bewildered in Bettendorf

Planning: To help you decide what should be done in this situation, list all the problems that can affect Buster or the writer's family. As you list them, ask yourself how serious they are. Are the problems great enough to warrant doing something as drastic as killing the dog? (In other words, are the problems serious enough to warrant changing the current policy of keeping the dog alive?)

The writer is naturally reluctant to have the dog put to sleep. Is killing the dog the only way to eliminate all the problems you have listed? What possible alternative solutions can you offer the writer to eliminate the problems or reduce their seriousness? Are these alternative solutions feasible? If there are some good alternative solutions, there's no need to take the drastic action of killing the dog.

Composing: Using the planning sheet, compose a letter to the dog owner in which you propose a solution to the problem and provide a logical rationale for your solution. Your letter should have the following features:

- An *introduction* restating the reader's question and expressing a recommendation about what action he should take.

- A *series of arguments* supporting your recommendation. Use the planning sheet to guide the development of the arguments. This part of your composition reviews the related problems and measures their significance.

(continues)

Figure 2–2. The Advice Columnist Assignment (*continued*)

- A *recognition of opposing arguments* fairly evaluating arguments counter to your own.
- A *conclusion* summarizing the current problem and restating the recommendation.
- It should be *polished* and *correct*.

Editing

Ask someone to read your letter and answer the following questions:

1. Does the writer take a definite position regarding the conflict?

2. Does the writer identify the problems?

3. Does the writer explain the extent of the problems?

4. Does the writer recognize the possible alternative solutions?

5. Has the writer evaluated the alternative solutions?

Use the comments made by your reader to guide the revisions you will make in your letter.

Karl: This dog smells really bad. Everyone in the family is embarrassed to bring friends home because of the smell. It has gotten into the furniture and stuff. That would be expensive to keep cleaning. And who would want to keep cleaning the furniture to get the smell out?

You: So, if we grant that Buster's bad smell is a big problem, couldn't the family do something small to reduce the bad smell? I know that if you put the dog to sleep and bury him, the smell will go away. But isn't there something less radical that you could do?

Renee: The kid could wash the dog a lot and spray the house with room freshener.

You: Okay. Is that a good solution?

Figure 2–3. Argument Planning Sheet

A. SOLUTION: What should be done in this situation?

B. What are the PROBLEMS that   In what way can the problems
   Buster and the family face?   be considered SERIOUS?

1.

2.

3.

4.

5.

C. What are the possible   Explain how these remedies are
   alternative solutions?   either GOOD or BAD solutions.

1.

2.

3.

4.

5.

Stanley: What kid is going give a dog a bath twice a week? And that begins to cost the family money, because you have to use special shampoo.

Freda: I have a dog, and I know that it is not good to bathe him that often. His skin will dry out, especially in winter. He'll be more miserable than ever.

Renee: But if the kid really loves the dog, he will be willing to take the trouble and maybe pay for the shampoo himself. It can't be that expensive.

An exchange like this is a necessary part of thinking thoroughly about the problem for which the writer seeks help. Students ask one another to support their claims. How significant is the problem? They challenge one another to consider alternative solutions. They immerse themselves in the *procedures* of arguing a policy question.

EPISODE 1.4. Equipped with the notes they took on the planning sheet as refined during the discussion, students begin writing their letter. The assignment handout outlines standards for writing a strong persuasive essay.

One of the benefits of debate is that it exposes the participants and the audience to at least two sides of the same question. In this case, one could construct reasonable arguments either to preserve the status quo (i.e., keep Buster alive) or to change the current situation (i.e., put Buster to sleep). While the writer who wants to change the current situation will point out the problems and their significance, the opponent might deny that any problems exist (e.g., *Buster doesn't smell bad at all*) or that they are not serious enough to require change. It seems in this situation that it would be hard to deny some of the problems (e.g., Buster either has his teeth or he doesn't), but someone could judge that the problems are not compelling enough to warrant radical action. Even if one were to admit that there are problems and that they are serious, it is possible to find workable solutions that will keep the dog alive, at least for a bit longer. The point is not to sponsor a "right" answer but to promote rational and thorough thinking about the problem.

There is a strong probability you will have a least one student who has experienced the emotional trauma of putting a beloved pet to sleep. This child might want to be excused from the discussion. In any case, select the language you use to discuss euthanasia carefully.

Stage 2. Applying Learned Procedures to a New Case

The case in Figure 2–4 simulates a problem with which students are probably familiar. The managers of a suburban shopping mall are worried about an apparent increase in injuries and retail thefts. One of the provocative elements is that teens are stereotyped as the source of some of the problems. The case includes a lot of information students can cite as evidence to support their claims: (1) testimonies from characters connected with the case, and (2) a summary of statistical data. Typically, writers support claims by drawing on three different types of evidence: examples, expert testimony, and statistical data.

Here students can cite examples from testimonies, but they need to consider whether a specific example is representative of a general trend or, if it isn't, whether it is compelling enough in itself to warrant change. Also, the reader will want to know the credentials of the source. Is the spokesperson an expert on the subject? What gives her or him the knowledge and authority to be considered an expert?

The statistical tables summarize (1) the number of injuries and retail thefts at the shopping mall and (2) the number of patrons over a four-year period. Insightful students will recognize that the two sets of numbers are interrelated: the increase in the number of crimes and injuries may be revealing, but the *rate* of increase may be more revealing.

This case emphasizes the deliberate consideration of different points of view. Throughout, students draw conclusions, support claims, evaluate rebuttals, and test the efficacy of plans. The testimonies reveal that not everyone agrees that there is a significant problem, what the source of any problem might be, and how to remedy any apparent problem. During discussions about the case, students should evaluate the perceptions and analyses of the characters who testify.

Figure 2–4. Security at the Mall Assignment

The managers of Heather Hills Mall have adopted a *new security policy*. Influenced by the recent rise in thefts and injuries, the managers have directed the security guards to:

- Not allow adolescents between the ages of 12 and 17 to assemble on Mall property, including parking lots, in groups of three or more. Adolescents who do not disperse will be arrested by local police for disturbing the peace and unlawful assembly.

- Encourage all shop owners to inspect the bags that adolescents carry out of a store.

- Stop any adolescent from skateboarding or in-line skating anywhere on the Mall property. If the adolescent persists, he or she will be arrested for disorderly conduct.

Questions for Reflection

- Are these new procedures necessary and justified? What are the *problems* that have prompted the managers to institute this new policy? How *significant* are the problems?

- Is the new policy necessary? Are the new procedures likely to do any good? Are the new procedures likely to be better than the practices of Mall security in the past?

- Is it likely that the new procedures will accomplish what the managers want—reduce thefts and injuries? How do you know?

- Will the new policy likely cause additional problems? Will the new policy result in benefits beyond the ones expected by the Mall managers?

The Data

Judge the new policy by looking at the relevant data:

1. The testimonies of people connected to the case, as collected in recent interviews.

(continues)

Figure 2–4. Security at the Mall Assignment (*continued*)

2. Tables of relevant statistical data (Tables 1 and 2, attached).

3. Study all the data before arriving at your own conclusions. Use the data to produce your written response to the case.

Writing About the Case: After you and your classmates have examined the data and thought about this situation, write to the managers of Heather Hills Mall to explain whether or not they should continue with the new security policy. In your composition:

- Summarize the current problem facing the managers of the Mall, and recommend whether or not they should follow the new security policy.

- Support your recommendation by pointing out and explaining relevant numbers and testimonies. What problems do you hope to reduce or eliminate? How big are these problems? Who is affected, and what is the impact?

- There will be some persons who don't agree with you. What is their position? Why do you think they're wrong?

- Summarize and restate your position about this situation at the Mall.

- Check your composition for correct spelling, grammar, and usage, as well as for neatness.

Testimonies

Ninian Q. Lyons (shopper, age 73): "I used to shop at the Heather Hills Mall, but I don't go there any more. The bands of teenagers who hang out at the Mall are intimidating. When I've gone there, young punks are often roving around in groups of six or more. You know they're up to no good. They make it difficult to pass. It is even difficult to get into the Mall, because skateboarders use the sidewalks and jump over curbs. I am afraid to death that

(*continues*)

Figure 2–4. Security at the Mall Assignment (*continued*)

I'm going to be run over. I'll tell you, I no longer feel comfortable going to the Mall. If they could get those teenagers under control, I'd consider going back."

Alberta Norbus (store manager, age 43): "I'm glad that they are going to stop the skateboarders, because they clearly pose a hazard to shoppers and workers. But it is not very practical to expect the store operators to inspect every bag of every teenage customer who comes into the store. We are a small operation and just can't afford the personnel that we would need to inspect bags. I'm not sure it would do any good, anyway. After all, the big-time shoplifters are the older 'professional' thieves. Although a person who is twenty-one is arrested only once, he may have shoplifted hundreds of times before getting caught; and his thefts may have been worth thousands of dollars each."

Rita Flambert (shopper, age 15): "I like to go to the Mall with three or four friends. We go there to shop and to walk around and meet people. We usually stop at the food court and get something to eat. But we mind our own business. We aren't shoplifting and we aren't causing anyone any problem. What are we supposed to do if five of us go to the Mall together? Split up into two groups? Why would we do that?"

Hilary Backstrom (parent, age 46): "I would prefer that my teenage son go to the Mall with friends. I can't be at the Mall with him, and he wouldn't want me around. When I drop him off, I like to know that he is with friends. Kids are very vulnerable these days. I don't like my son to be alone. There is safety in numbers, and I would like to see him at the Mall with two or three friends."

Ezekiel Thrommer (skateboarder, age 14): "It's true that I was injured when I was skateboarding at the Mall three-months ago. Near the main entrance there are ramps that cut into the curb. My friends and I like to use the ramps and

(continues)

Figure 2–4. Security at the Mall Assignment (*continued*)

we like to jump the curb. There was no sign posted that said we couldn't skateboard. I fell when I jumped the curb and I shattered my elbow. I had two surgeries, and the doctors installed a metal pin in my elbow. My dad is suing the Mall for not taking any measures to prevent such injuries from occurring. If we win the law suit, my dad is buying me a car."

Hogart Thisby (director of security, age 39): "In the last four years we have had a lot of security concerns. Our merchants report increases in thefts in their stores. There has also been an increase in other thefts outside of stores. For example, parents have had baby strollers stolen, and kids have reported bicycles stolen. Teens tend to congregate in the Mall. I can tell you this: a lot of older shoppers don't feel comfortable around these teenagers. The teens tend to be loud and hang out in groups. To the older shopper, any large and loud group of teenagers seems like a gang. I must also note that we have had an increase in the number of injuries reported on the Mall property. These injuries involve all kinds of accidents and mishaps, but they include injuries to teenagers who skateboard or in-line skate on the property."

Table 1
Growth of the
Heather Hills Mall Over Four Years

YEAR	NUMBER OF STORES	NUMBER OF PATRONS PER YEAR
Four Years Ago	50	278,000
Three Years Ago	78	356,000
Two Years Ago	84	380,000
Last Year	124	551,000

(*continues*)

Figure 2–4. Security at the Mall Assignment (*continued*)

Table 2
Number of Thefts and Injuries
per Year per Age Group

Ages	Four Years Ago		Three Years Ago		Two Years Ago		Last Year	
	Injuries	Arrest for Theft	Injuries	Arrest for Theft	Injuries	Arrest for Theft	Injuries	Arrest for Theft
12–17	12	26	18	41	20	58	27	102
18–25	10	30	14	32	15	34	20	51
26–40	8	21	5	26	9	24	12	23
41–65	9	13	8	12	7	16	8	12
65–older	16	2	19	3	20	4	23	2

EPISODE 2.1.   Have students, independently, read the case, including all the testimonies. Ask them to study the proposed new policy and the summary tables of statistical information.

EPISODE 2.2.   Have students, in small groups of three or four, share their decisions and analyses. It's unlikely that the thinking in any group will be identical, but each group should try to reach a consensus; it prompts them to evaluate claims, interpret data, and propose remedies. They should use the questions for reflection included in the case analysis to guide their work.

EPISODE 2.3.   Hold a whole-class discussion. Ask a spokesperson for each group to share the group's analysis. There is likely to be healthy disagreement; students will be forced to consider opposing views and defend their positions. This discussion may take up an entire class meeting, and students should take notes about their own conclusions and about the reasonable opposition. Their talk is an oral rehearsal, an opportunity to generate new ideas for the substance of their writing.

EPISODE 2.4. Have students write a draft response, share it with peers, revise it, and edit it. Peer review and revision should reflect the standards that were established as students grappled with the case.

Summing Up

A structured process approach to teaching argument, as modeled in this chapter, emphasizes the use of problem-based activities. The problems are ones adolescents recognize as common to their own experience. Anyone puzzling over a problem is frustrated if there isn't enough information to solve it; the cases include the relevant information. The process includes frequent opportunities for students to talk to each other. Small-group work can be a waste of instructional time if it is not managed skillfully. The groups need a specific task, time parameters, and an expected product. Large-group discussion must invite participation and even when contentious remain civil and rational. You need to listen actively, invite opposition, summarize the exchanges, and not insist on a predetermined decision. At the end of the process, students should be able to write fully developed arguments, and they should be able to explain to someone else how they thought about the case and how they created their argument.

Extensions

Students are likely to care deeply about issues that affect them, such as school security (or the administration's obsession with security), limited school parking, and similar community issues, as well as the management of their favorite professional sports franchise. Invite learners to apply their knowledge of written argument to advance their own propositions related to the local problems or issues they care most about.

3

Considering Competing
Points of View

Our model of argument recognizes opposing points of view. Too often, the combatants in a heated oral exchange concentrate on strengthening their own position without considering the merits of the opposing position. It is difficult for adolescents to break away from this competitive model and embrace the inherent honesty of considering competing points of view and admitting the merits of those views when warranted. The explicit recognition, accurate representation, and fair evaluation of opposing views marks a writer as a fair-minded person whose ideas are worthy of consideration. This appearance of fair-mindedness bespeaks credibility. (Aristotle calls this quality *extrinsic ethos*: in addition to knowing what you are talking about, you want to appear that you know what you are talking about.)

The three lessons in this chapter, which progress from simple to complex, teach students how to recognize and assess competing points of view on debatable issues. Each lesson can be connected to a specific work of literature or to a possible thematic unit of study.

Stage 1. Weighing Financial Reward Against Sentimental Value

In this activity, students argue whether (and how) to dispose of a cherished family heirloom. Selling it would give family members money they really need, but they would lose an emblem of family identity, pride, and hope. Students learn how to represent and evaluate an opposing point of view. (The activity can be used in connection with August Wilson's *The Piano Lesson* and Alice Walker's short story "Everyday Use." It's also a gateway lesson for a unit of instruction connecting several works of literature about the formation of identity or the tensions between monetary gain and moral and esthetic values.)

Students, in pairs, role-play a brother and sister who disagree about what to do with a family heirloom. On the surface, each has a reasonable position, and the students must first represent one of the positions fairly and accurately in a letter to their sibling. Then, in another letter from and to third parties, they weigh the competing arguments and show that while there are merits to both recommendations, one has more advantages and fewer disadvantages—this is called a *comparative advantage analysis*.

Both letters are drafted, reviewed, revised, and edited. Classmates who were assigned the opposite point of view are the best choice for peer reviewers; the initial letters are addressed to them, and they will be especially sensitive to the way their partner represents their point of view in the second letter.

EPISODE 1.1. Distribute the assignment (Figure 3–1) and have students read it on their own. Divide the class into pairs of students, one taking Steve's point of view, the other, Sue's. Then have everyone formulate an argument asserting why her or his position on how to dispose of the inheritance is reasonable, and express that point of view in a letter to their sibling.

Figure 3–1. Batter Up!

Backstory

Steve and Sue Witts are brother and sister. They grew up together in Titusville, New Jersey, a town considered a suburb of New York City. As adults, Steve and Sue drifted apart. Steve continued to live in Titusville, but Sue married and moved to Fremont, Indiana. Their mother, Elvira Hoppsdale Witts, died when Steve and Sue were very young.

After completing an associate's degree at Titusville Community College, Steve opened a sports memorabilia shop. He specializes in the sale of vintage baseball cards. Steve's shop did quite well for a time, but baseball enthusiasm began to flag and sales of sports memorabilia in general declined. Steve now has large outstanding debts and may lose his shop. Steve is especially concerned about being evicted from his property and losing all his assets to the Titusville Equity Bank, whose president is Benton Whicket, a man whom Steve's father detested.

When Sue and Steve were quite young, the Titusville Equity Bank and Benton Whicket repossessed the Witts' home, forcing the family and their meager possessions into the street. Dale Witts was certain that being thrown out into the dreadful New Jersey winter led to the pneumonia that eventually took his wife Elvira's life. For the remainder of his life, Dale Witts held Benton Whicket responsible for his wife's death.

Sue Witts has had trouble of her own. She married a New Jersey cab driver named Lance Storm. After six months of marriage and during the fourth month of her pregnancy, Sue lost her husband when the cab he was driving fell off an expressway ramp and Lance died. Sue was left to raise her son Claude Storm by herself. The mother and son struggled financially. As Claude grew older, however, he excelled in baseball and took great interest in his mother's stories about her father Dale "Buck" Witts, a long-time

(continues)

Figure 3–1. Batter Up! (*continued*)

minor league baseball player who served a brief stint with the New York Yankees in 1964. The grim dreariness and painful poverty of Claude's life was somehow tolerable when he thought that his own grandfather had been an accomplished baseball player who had played with some players who are now enshrined in the Baseball Hall of Fame in Cooperstown.

Recently, Dale "Buck" Witts, Claude's grandfather and the father of Steve and Sue, died after a long battle with cancer. He had little to leave his children, but he did bequeath to them a baseball bat he had used during the brief time he was called up from the minors to play with the New York Yankees. Every member of the 1964 New York Yankees, including Dale "Buck" Witts himself, signed the bat. Among the signatures are those of Mickey Mantle, Yogi Berra, Tony Kubek, Bobby Richardson, Elston Howard, Roger Maris, and Whitey Ford. The bat proves that Dale "Buck" Witts indeed played with some of the greatest players of the game.

Steve and Sue were happy to inherit the baseball bat, but they each have a different idea about what to do with it. Steve realizes that this rare baseball bat can fetch as much as $15,000 at auction. With his share of the sale, Steve can pay his debts, keep his business, and show the insidious Benton Whicket that the Witts are no longer his victims. Sue sees things another way. She doesn't want to part with the artifact for any amount of money. She is willing to work twice as hard and face continued hardship rather than sell this important family heirloom. To Sue, the baseball bat represents a high point in the family's history. No one else in the world has any business owning this rare and private artifact. The bat will also instill in Claude a sense of hope, promise, and pride. How can she sell something so precious?

(continues)

Figure 3–1. Batter Up! (*continued*)

Put It in Writing

Since Steve and Sue live far apart and have very little money, they need to try to reach an agreement by mail.

1. Imagine how Steve and Sue each think about their dilemma. Write the letter you imagine either Steve or Sue (whoever's point of view you were assigned) writes to the other.

2. After you have written the letter, exchange it with a classmate who has written a letter from the opposite point of view. Study this second position, and judge which position seems the most convincing.

3. Imagine you know both Sue and Steve and hate to see them at odds. Write a second letter, this one to their aunt, Doris Witts Carter, who can help Sue and Steve resolve their differences. Your letter should:

   - Begin by summarizing the problem and making a recommendation.

   - Represent fairly and accurately the argument of the sibling with whom you least agree.

   - Represent fairly and accurately the argument of the sibling with whom you most agree.

   - Explain how you have concluded that one argument offers the family the most advantage and the least disadvantage. Or you might find the positions of both Steve and Sue lacking and offer another possibility for resolving the conflict.

EPISODE 1.2.   Have students exchange letters with a classmate who took the opposing point of view and examine the opposing arguments. Equipped with this knowledge, each student should then write a second letter, as a disinterested third party, summarizing the problem and making a recommendation. The body of the letter should represent the arguments of both characters fairly and accurately and offer a judgment about the relative merits of the two views, concluding that one offers greater advantages or that neither the brother nor the sister offered a compelling argument; in the latter case an alternative course of action should be suggested.

Stage 2. Deciding Between Two Choices

In this lesson, students consider how gender roles, connections with our parents, and loyalty to a place can influence our decisions. It could be used to introduce a thematic unit connecting several works of fiction and/or nonfiction dealing with identity.

EPISODE 2.1. Hand out and discuss the assignment in Figure 3–2.

Figure 3–2. The Sad Case of Larry Farqwardt

Backstory

One could say that fourteen-year-old Larry Farqwardt, of Floodrock, Illinois, is the product of a "mixed marriage." In Floodrock, baseball fans root for either the Cardinals or the Cubs.

Larry's father, Glenn Farqwardt, has been a lifelong St. Louis Cardinals fan. Glenn grew up in St. Louis, in "the Hill," a neighborhood that has produced some famed major league baseball players. When Glenn was growing up, the Cardinals were perennial contenders for the National League pennant, while the Cubs were the doormat of the league. The Cubs couldn't do anything right, like the time they traded future Hall of Fame outfielder Lou Brock for journeyman pitcher Ernie Broglio. The infamous trade is an embarrassment to Cubs fans to this day. All Glenn's friends in the neighborhood were also enthusiastic Cardinals fans. A highlight of Glenn's childhood was his father's taking him to game four of the 1967 World Series to see the Cardinals defeat the Boston Red Sox 6–0, with Bob Gibson throwing a five-hit shutout. Glenn has remained passionately loyal

(continues)

Figure 3–2. The Sad Case of Larry Farqwardt *(continued)*

to the Cardinals. He cannot understand how anyone can have any passion for the Cubs. Glenn likes to say that he supports two major league teams: the Cardinals, obviously, and whoever happens to be playing the Cubs.

Larry's mother, Myrna Farqwardt, grew up on the north side of Chicago, where she became, predictably, an avid Cubs fan. Her great-uncle, Johnny Fungillini, had been a bat boy for the Cubs and knew a number of great players personally, including Gabby Hartnett and Stan Hack. Myrna often argues with her husband about the relative merits of the two Central Division teams. She likes to recall that before the 1972 season, the Cardinals traded future Hall of Fame pitcher Steve Carlton to Philadelphia for Rick Wise—probably one of the worst trades in baseball history. Myrna is such a loyal fan she attended a Cubs pennant-race game on the same day as her grandmother's funeral.

Mom or Pop?

This year the annual midwinter Cubs convention and the Cardinals convention have been scheduled for the same weekend, in downtown Chicago and downtown St. Louis, respectively. The Cubs fans will meet at the Days Inn on Lake Shore Drive in Chicago, while the Cardinals Convention will be at the Adams Mark Hotel, in downtown St. Louis. Myrna Farqwardt plans to attend the Cubs convention and has an extra ticket for Larry. Glenn will attend the Cardinals convention and he too has an extra ticket for Larry.

Larry cannot attend both conventions, since they will meet at the same time, at hotels that are approximately 300 miles apart. If he doesn't join his mother, she will be bitterly disappointed. She has always hoped her son would join her in being a Cubs fan. She's told him that if he goes to the Cubs convention, he'll see Cubs greats like Ernie Banks, Billy Williams, and Glenn Beckert. Larry's father will be equally upset if Larry declines his invitation. At the Cardinals

(continues)

Figure 3–2. The Sad Case of Larry Farqwardt *(continued)*

convention, Larry could meet Curt Flood, Julian Javier, and Lou Brock. Since Larry is only fourteen years old, staying home alone all weekend is not an option. What should Larry do?

Discussion Questions

1. If Larry chooses one invitation over the other, does that mean he is choosing one parent over the other and identifying himself with that parent? Does his decision mean that he rejects one parent? Explain.

2. If Larry chooses one invitation over the other, does that mean that he has identified himself with one team and one city? Explain.

3. Will Larry's decision have long-lasting consequences? How would his decision affect his future?

4. To what extent is Larry able to make a choice freely, without the control of external forces?

5. Is there a way to decide objectively that one convention is better than the other?

6. Is there a way to reach a compromise? How would the compromise work? Why would a compromise have value?

Put It in Writing

Write a response to Larry and his parents. Draw from your initial notes and any notes you took during group and class discussions. In your response be sure to:

- Summarize the problem in enough detail that someone unfamiliar with the discussion knows what's at stake.

- Restate the wishes and rationale of one parent accurately and thoroughly.

- Restate the wishes and rational of the second parent accurately and thoroughly.

(continues)

Figure 3–2. The Sad Case of Larry Farqwardt *(continued)*

- Evaluate the relative merits of the position of each parent.

- Recommend Larry go with either one parent or the other, or present a compromise. (This recommendation may precede or follow an analysis of the competing positions.)

- If you offer a compromise, describe how it would work and explain why it is better than siding with one or the other parent.

EPISODE 2.2.   Have students, individually, jot down answers to the discussion questions included in the assignment (be sure you give them enough time). Then ask them to share their responses in small groups (set a reasonable time limit). Finally, let them exchange ideas as a class. In the class discussion, prompt students to be logical. When someone makes a claim, ask, *Why would you say that?* or *How did you arrive at that conclusion?* When someone cites details of the case as evidence, ask, *So what?* prompting him or her to explain or interpret how the claim must necessarily follow from the evidence. These common interchanges alert students that a skeptical audience might want to know why they are making a claim and how the evidence demonstrates that the claim is valid.

EPISODE 2.3.   Have students use the ideas they've generated and discussed to draft a written response. Then ask them to be one another's editors, focusing their comments on the degree to which the writer has honored the requirements for a thorough and logical argument.

Stage 3. Representing Several Points of View

This activity is a bit more complicated than the prior two. This time students take the position of someone with whose arguments they don't entirely agree. (Some students won't feel comfortable advocating a position not their own. It may help to suggest they think of it as playing a part in a play. Also, for the activity to work, students need to know they can play the roles without fear of ridicule.) The goal is for students to recognize and evaluate the positions of competing characters. Conscientious thinkers don't advance an argument in a vacuum; they recognize the various sides in a dispute, represent them fairly, and evaluate the relative merits of each view. The activity can be used in connection with fiction or nonfiction that explores equality, inclusion, exclusion, and accommodation.

EPISODE 3.1. Hand out the brief narrative and simple data summary in Figure 3–3. Read the case aloud (or have students read it silently) and ask for volunteers to summarize the essential problem; students need to be able to explain in their own words what the dispute is about.

Figure 3–3. The Line for the Restroom

Backstory

The Creeksville Crows are a minor league baseball team that draws several thousand people to local games. The Creeksville Coliseum, the Crows' home ballpark, is celebrating its 75th anniversary this year. Habakuk Thompson, the founder of the Crows, built the coliseum long ago, when more men than women attended baseball games; consequently the ratio of men's to women's restrooms is three to one; there are a total of nine men's restrooms and three women's restrooms. Each men's room can accommodate up to fifteen men (ten urinals, five stalls), while each women's room can only accommodate five women (five stalls). This means that 135 men but only fifteen women can use a restroom at any given time.

When Ya Gotta Go, Ya Gotta Go

Jane Jurraczyk has been a fan of the Crows for several years and faithfully attends each home game. Several thousand

(continues)

Figure 3–3. The Line for the Restroom (*continued*)

fans were in attendance at last week's game, on an unusually hot day. Jane tried to combat the heat by drinking several soft drinks; she then left her seat to go to the restroom. Along the way, she passed three men's rooms before finally reaching the women's room. Jane stood in line behind twenty-five other women. Twenty minutes later, she had advanced only ten spots in line. Jane also noticed there was no line at the nearest men's room. Desperate for relief, she went in, and four other women followed. When they tried to leave they were blocked by a group of outraged men. Security guards separated the groups before any fights broke out, but a few of the women insisted on speaking to the owner about the discrepancy between the number of men's and women's restrooms. The current Crows' owner, Gabriel Thompson, has scheduled a meeting to discuss whether he should provide equal accommodations for men and women and, if so, how best to do so.

Focus Question

What should be done to provide adequate and equitable restroom facilities for men and women at the Creeksville Coliseum?

Procedure

The class has been divided into six groups. Your group will represent the views of a specific person (see the character descriptions that follow) and prepare an argument to support a particular course of action. Try to anticipate what each other character may say in response. What arguments can you develop to persuade the others to consider your point of view?

Put It in Writing

After the class has discussed possible solutions to the problem, you will each write your own letter to the ballpark owner explaining what you think should be done about the limited bathroom facilities for women. Your argument should state the grounds for your recommendation and explain how you

(*continues*)

Figure 3–3. The Line for the Restroom (*continued*)

interpreted any relevant data or testimony. While presenting your own opinion, be sure to take into account the opinions expressed by others at the meeting.

CREEKSVILLE COLISEUM Quick Facts	
Seating Capacity	5,062
Total Season Attendance:	182,800
Average Game Attendance:	2,649
Percent of Female Attendees:	37
Percent of Male Attendees:	63
Average Concession Transaction:	$7.75

Character Descriptions

Jane Jurraczyk: Mother of three, she has a fourth child on the way. She is a loyal fan of the Crows, usually patient under any circumstance. Her only goal is *to explain* that she entered the men's room simply because she could not wait any longer. She doesn't have a particular solution in mind, except that she would like the club ownership to be a little more flexible in how the restroom facilities can be used. Jane would like everyone to discuss the matter in a very polite and civilized manner. She feels very uncomfortable being the center of controversy.

Bertha Bartolomeo: Bertha followed Jane Jurraczyk into the men's restroom because she was genuinely upset about watching men enter and leave their restroom while she was made to wait. Her immediate goal is to convince the owner that it is only fair that he change the restrooms *to provide equal accommodations* for all. Many women now attend the Crows' games, and it is only fair that they be provided with adequate bathroom facilities. Bertha doesn't want to reduce the number of men's restrooms; she wants adequate new

(*continues*)

Figure 3–3. The Line for the Restroom (*continued*)

restrooms installed for women, whatever the cost. She feels she has a constitutional right to equal access to public restrooms. Bertha can be loud, and she will not tolerate any patronizing or evasive responses from the owner or timid compromises from other women.

Phyllis Cobden: Phyllis, or Phyl as she prefers to be called, is outraged at the disparity between the way men and women are treated everywhere, and she sees this incident as an example of how society oppresses women. She is willing to take this issue as far as it will go. She knows what *equal* means, and she sees no reason to wait. She wants an *immediate solution*: as soon as the meeting ends, the owner must designate six of the existing men's restrooms as women's restrooms, so an equal number of men and women can be accommodated at any given time. She wants men to realize that times have changed: they cannot rely on attitudes and practices from seventy-five years ago to guide their current policy. Phyllis will take every opportunity to identify the many instances of sexual bias in the community. That no women are on the Creeksville Crows team or part of its management are two glaring examples.

Al Bludgens: Al was in the restroom when the women entered and was very upset about this invasion of privacy. He claims that there is only one women's room to every three men's rooms because the ballpark is *no place for women*. He believes baseball can be a violent and vulgar game, played by men for the entertainment of men. He sees the coliseum as an asylum from the frivolities of nagging women. This bastion of maleness has been invaded by women who don't understand the game and create a distraction. To make matters worse, he can't even use the men's restroom without being interrupted by a group of impatient women who have facilities of their own. According to Al, this current controversy is just another example of women's lack of patience, strength, and common sense.

(*continues*)

Figure 3–3. The Line for the Restroom (*continued*)

Bruce Fairmont: Bruce doesn't see any problem. There are a total of twelve restrooms, all of which should become unisex bathrooms available to both men *and* women. What's the big deal? Body parts and bodily functions are natural and nothing to be ashamed of. Men and women sharing restroom facilities is common in many parts of the world. At various festivals and outdoor events, men and women use portable accommodations, separated from each other only by a thin sheet of plastic.

Gabriel Thompson: Gabriel, the team owner, is very concerned; he has a very big problem on his hands. Building new restrooms is expensive, a cost he did not anticipate in his budget. It is also quite costly to renovate existing men's rooms into women's rooms. He wants to solve the problem as cheaply as he can. Gabriel is also concerned about his public image and that of the Creeksville Crows. He can't afford to make a lot of enemies. He doesn't want nasty letters to the editor of the local newspaper, picketing, or boycotts of the ball games. He will reason that *comparable* does not always mean *numerically equal*. He will remind everyone that it is still true that far more men than women attend the ball games. He figures that the women may need one more restroom at most, if he can afford it.

EPISODE 3.2.   Form six groups and assign each group a role. Have each group study the role description, formulate that character's argument (they should take notes, not rely on memory), and select a spokesperson.

EPISODE 3.3.   Hold a community forum:

- Have the spokesperson from one group present an argument (uninterrupted), noting any significant downsides and offering a solution.

- Have the spokesperson from a second group paraphrase the argument of the previous speaker, confirm that the paraphrase is accurate, and then present his or her own argument.

- Continue in this way until each group has presented its argument.

- Open the floor to all group members, who can ask questions, challenge statements, and present rebuttals.

EPISODE 3.4.   Have students, individually, prepare a written argument based on either a stock issues approach or a comparative advantage analysis. The key element is acknowledging the opposing views and positioning the writer's argument within the larger conversation.

Extensions

A look around your own school and community will reveal many regrettable inequities, some based on gender, some based on physical challenges, some based on other biases. For a deeper sense of involvement, students can put the same powers of analysis to work researching and addressing any of these inequities.

Constructing Gateways

> Theories of discourse, inquiry, learning, and teaching are useless
> if we cannot invent the activities that will engage our students in
> using, and therefore learning, the strategies essential to certain
> writing tasks. These activities provide the circumstances and sup-
> port that enable them to use strategies that they would otherwise
> not be able to use. Because writing involves both substantive and
> affective purposes, our activities will have to involve students in
> appropriate strategies of inquiry and ways of generating discourse
> features. I refer to these as *gateway activities*. (Hillocks 1995, 149)

Gateway activities tap relevant prior knowledge or help students
build knowledge necessary for the task at hand. They also rely on
student interaction: students learn to write by talking as well as
writing. The lessons in the previous chapters are all gateway activities to help students learn to write arguments: assert and support
generalizations, interpret evidence, respond to rebuttals, and weigh
the relative advantages of several options.

Sometimes, as in Chapter 3, the activities are based on personal
experiences and enthusiasms or parallel the literature students will
study. But sources for gateway activities that immerse students in
debatable situations and issues are all around us: movies, television
shows, songs, and other media. The daily newspaper is a gold mine
of contentious cases.

The activities in this chapter are based on newspaper accounts of contentious situations. It's best to select stories that do not reveal a strong bias (or to alter them so the sides are more balanced). Also, avoid problems on a grand scale, like suppressing nuclear proliferation or slowing climate change. When students are learning to argue logically and civilly, it is more productive if they grapple with problems closer to their daily lives.

Following these steps will help you construct gateway activities:

1. Identify the *target outcome* by expressing what you would like learners to be able to do as a result of their learning. This requires envisioning what achievement of the target outcome looks like.

2. Complete a *task analysis*: What do the learners need to know? What do they need to be able to do?

3. Through reflection and informal assessment, gauge the learners' *prior knowledge* and *interests* relative to the target outcome.

4. Formulate an *appropriate problem* that taps prior knowledge and interests and will prompt necessary processes/new learning. Problems can take many forms, since every writing situation is unique. (A narrative writing problem? Imagine hiding between two dumpsters in a dark alley. The sound of footsteps gets closer and closer. Why are you hiding, and who is approaching? What will happen? Or, a problem about a proposed purchase might require analyzing costs and benefits.)

5. Provide *supportive data* learners need in order to work with the given problem (or design a process in which learners assemble their own data).

6. Structure a *small-group task* with a specific goal, an opportunity for all learners to participate, a time limit, a dynamic element that prompts interaction (like attempting to reach consensus), and an expectation for sharing with the larger group.

7. Specify a *context* and a *forum* for the entire class to discuss the problem.

8. Decide how you will *summarize the activities* and highlight the agreements, commitments, or general conclusions of the group.

9. Provide a *transition* from the preparatory activities to the subsequent learning by explicitly noting connections and explaining how procedures apply to a product, a task, or a performance.

10. Build in a *self-reflection* component that encourages the learners to be consciously aware of the procedures they followed as they investigated a problem, formulated conclusions, and completed a product or performance.

Here's an example of how a trivial news story might become the basis for an argumentation writing problem. After Super Bowl XLI (2006), newspapers reported that a Bears fan lost a bet on the outcome of the game and was obliged to change his name to Peyton Manning. One could use the story as is to explore themes of honor and duty or fictionalize it into something more complex. Perhaps a young woman named Siobhan Murphy loses a bet, made when she was drunk, that requires her to change her name to Adewale Ogunleye. If Siobhan honors her obligation, her parents and siblings will be upset and her husband might leave her. With the stakes raised, the problem prompts learners to examine concepts related to identity.

The idea for a problem may be an individual inspiration, but a fully realized gateway activity is best created *collaboratively*. Just as students better understand concepts and produce better writing when they interact with their peers, a gateway activity will be made richer and more appealing by the contributions of the members of a team as they detail procedures, devise a rubric, evaluate group work, and so on.

Stage 1. Examining Personal Responsibility

EPISODE 1.1. Introduce the activity in Figure 4–1, which is based on a real news story about a small-town councilwoman who offered to care for her neighbors' dog while they were on vacation. When they got back, the councilwoman contritely confessed that the dog

Figure 4–1. The Case of the Runaway Dog

The Gorman family (Paul, Carla, and their children, Sonna, twelve; Freddie, nine; and Ben, eight) are leaving their hometown of Hatboro, Pennsylvania, for an extended vacation. They have a three-year-old Maltese named Pancho. Although the dog is technically Sonna's (he was a present from her parents for her tenth birthday), he is attached to every member of the family. Although Carla is primarily the one who feeds, walks, and grooms Pancho, every member of the family shows the dog affection. Pancho is very affectionate with family members but shy around strangers. They are worried about boarding the dog in a kennel for two weeks.

A Good Neighbor to the Rescue

Grace Horsham lives alone across the street from the Gorman family. During a casual conversation while Grace and Paul are each carrying garbage to the curb, Paul mentions the upcoming two-week vacation and how worried they are because they can't take Pancho with them. Grace says she enjoys seeing the dog play in front of the Gorman home and will be happy to keep the dog at her home for two weeks. At first, Paul is hesitant to impose, since he doesn't know Grace very well; but having someone in the neighborhood care for the dog is appealing. He asks the other family members what they think, and they decide to pay Grace twenty dollars a day to care for the dog. Grace is a retired accountant. Although she is a councilwoman on the Hatboro City Council and attends council and committee meetings, she is home for the greater part of each day. The arrangement seems ideal.

Things Go Wrong

While the Gorman family is away, Carla calls Grace to check on how she is getting along with Pancho. Grace tearfully tells Ms. Gorman that on the previous evening, Pancho dug his way under the fence in her yard and disappeared. She fears the dog has wandered far away and may have been picked up by some

(continues)

Figure 4–1. The Case of the Runaway Dog (*continued*)

one who won't be able to identify the owner, because she took Pancho's collar off when she bathed him and he escaped without his I.D. tags. She tells Carla she has filed a report with the local police and they are on the lookout. The Gorman family is stunned by the news. The children are heartbroken, and Paul says angrily that Grace was careless and thoughtless in not minding the dog properly and allowing it outside unattended with no collar and tags.

The Prodigal Returns

Two weeks after the family returns from vacation, Sonna passes Grace's house, thinks she hears Pancho's familiar bark but decides her imagination is playing tricks on her because she misses Pancho so much. Then Carla Gorman's sister Irene, who lives in nearby Telford, tells Carla she saw a dog that looked just like Pancho in a dog groomer's shop in Telford. Paul wonders whether someone from Telford found Pancho and kept him without reporting the stray dog to the police. A week later, Irene sees someone walking the dog down the street. She takes a picture of the dog and the woman walking him with the camera in her cellphone and sends it to Carla. The person walking the dog looks very much like Grace Horsham, but is actually her sister Hope Horsham, who also lives in Telford. Paul Gorman shows Hatboro police officers the photo of Hope Horsham and the Pancho lookalike.

Grace Faces the Music

After a brief investigation by the Hatboro and the Telford police, Grace Horsham admits that she intentionally took the dog to her sister's home in Telford and lied to the Gorman family and to the Hatboro police about his whereabouts. Grace is arrested for filing a false police report and for tampering with evidence. She makes the following statement before posting bail:

I know I could have gone about this in another way, but I was acting in the best interest of the little dog. Over the last

(*continues*)

Figure 4–1. The Case of the Runaway Dog (*continued*)

two years I saw how the family neglected him. They left him unattended in the yard for long periods of time, even in the rain and snow and bitter cold. I heard him crying to be allowed into the house. The few times a family member walked the dog past my house, I noticed his coat was all matted and dirty. When they left the dog with me for their vacation, he was infested with fleas, and the sores where he scratched himself were infected. I brought the dog to the vet for a flea treatment and examination. The vet had to give the dog an IV with an antibiotic to fight the infection and dehydration. I paid the vet 150 dollars. Knowing how he would suffer, maybe even die, if he returned to the Gorman family, I took matters into my own hands and placed the dog in a safer and more nurturing environment. I think any sensitive person would do what I did.

While Paul and Carla Gorman admit they had been battling a flea infestation in their home, they say Grace is exaggerating Pancho's condition. They insist they are a very loving family who have cared very much for Pancho and are eager for him to come home. Since the police cannot confiscate Pancho as they could stolen property like a bicycle or a computer, the dog will remain with Hope Horsham until the case is settled.

Grace Horsham and her sister Hope will soon have to face a judge in court. The charges are serious: falsifying a police report and tampering with evidence for Grace, concealing evidence for Hope. If convicted, Grace could go to jail for ten years; Hope could go to jail for a year. The central question for the judge is this: *What should happen to Pancho, to the members of the Gorman family, to their neighbor Grace Horsham, and to her sister Hope Horsham?*

Put It in Writing

As you consider this case, imagine the arguments the following people will make: Grace and Hope Horsham; Carla Gorman; a Hatboro police officer; and the neighbor who lives next door to

(*continues*)

Figure 4–1. The Case of the Runaway Dog (*continued*)

the Gormans. As you imagine these arguments, take notes and talk about the case with a classmate, a friend, or a family member. Then organize your ideas to help you to remember them.

In a letter to Judge Howard Hackney, explain what you think should happen to Pancho, to Grace and Hope Horsham, and to the Gorman family:

- In an *introduction*, show Judge Hackney that you are aware of the problem facing Pancho, the Gorman family, their neighbor Grace Horsham, and her sister Hope Horsham. Summarize the case and preview the discussion that will follow.

- In a *series of paragraphs*, represent fairly the argument of each side in the dispute, whether you agree with the argument or not.

- Make your recommendation for resolving the dispute. *Support* your recommendation with relevant information and explain how the information is significant.

- Conclude by briefly reviewing the problem and recommendation.

You'll probably make several attempts at writing your letter before you are satisfied with the finished product. Be sure to get some editorial help before you submit your final version.

had run away and could not be found. Later, the neighbors discovered the councilwoman was hiding the dog at her sister's home in a nearby town (Blumenthal 2008).

The story appeals to students because it features a cute dog and an authority figure acting badly, but there is no doubt who is at fault, so it needed a rewrite to make it debatable. Perhaps the mayor believed she was saving the dog from abuse and neglect. The students' job is to evaluate the competing views, analyze the case in writing, and make a final judgment.

This lesson may be used in connection with themes related to personal responsibility in works like "The Devil and Daniel Webster," by Stephen Vincent Benét; *The Odyssey*, by Homer; "The Man That Corrupted Hadleyburg" and *The Adventures of Huckleberry*

Finn, by Mark Twain; *The Red Kayak*, by Priscilla Cummings; "The Road Not Taken," by Robert Frost; *Twelve Angry Men*, by Reginald Rose; and "To Those of My Sisters Who Kept Their Naturals," by Gwendolyn Brooks. (See www.coe.uga.edu/~smago/VirtualLibrary/ Unit_Outlines.htm#Responsibility for more possibilities.)

EPISODE 1.2. Have students, in small groups, imagine what Grace Horsham, Hope Horsham, Carla Gorman, a local police officer, and a disinterested but observant neighbor think should happen to Pancho and whether they think anyone should be punished. Each small group then represents in writing what one these characters would say.

EPISODE 1.3. Have a representative from each group share the assigned character's point of view while the rest of the class takes notes. (Or have each group post their written statement on a wikispace that students consult when creating their individual responses.)

EPISODE 1.4. Have the students, as a class, analyze, challenge, and request evidence for each character's claims. The following composite of actual responses by sixth graders is representative:

Stephania: The Gorman family should get Pancho back, and Grace should go to jail for ten years. Her sister should go to jail, too, because she did not tell anyone.

Miriam: If the family did mistreat the dog, Grace and her sister should get the dog and no one would go to jail.

C.J.: The dog should go to the shelter, and Grace should go to jail for three months, because she lied to the police.

Emily: Grace should go to jail for ten years, her sister for one year. Find out if the dog was not cared for and should maybe go to a shelter.

Dom: Grace should go to jail for ten years because she filed a false police report, and mostly because she stole the dog. Hope should go to jail for one year for not telling the truth.

Jayson: The dog should go to an animal shelter, and Grace should go to jail for two and a half years for lying and stealing the dog. They didn't kill the dog.

Beth: They should not go to jail, and the dog should go back to the Gorman family.

Michael: The two sisters should go to jail. They didn't tell the police the dog was being abused and just stole him.

Meg: I don't think Grace thought the dog was treated badly, because everyone said the dog was affectionate to the members of the family. I'm not sure the dog was neglected. Grace is someone who lied, and maybe this is a habit for her. Can she be trusted to tell the truth? The facts don't add up.

Reynaldo: Grace should go to jail for two to five years, and do one to two years of community service for lying to the Gorman family and to the police and for stealing the dog. Pancho should go back to the Gorman family. Hope should have one to two years of community service.

Dee: Grace and the Gorman family should go to jail, and the dog goes to another family. If you believe Grace, the dog was neglected.

Bill: Grace should go to jail for five years. The dog should go to Gormans' relatives so they could visit him. Hope should get one year in jail.

You might stir up the discussion by saying something like, "You all seem to value honesty, which is good. But if I lied to protect a Jewish family from being detected by the Gestapo in Nazi Germany, would I deserve to be punished for lying? Maybe I should be honored."

EPISODE 1.5. Drawing from notes from discussions, students draft, revise, and edit their individual responses.

Stage 2. Examining Bias

This lesson was also inspired by a news story, about a group of teenage friends who set up a Wiffle ball field in a vacant lot in their neighborhood and played many hours every day until the neighbors complained about the noise and even about the teens' presence

(Applebome 2008). Again, this fictionalized version diminishes the bias in the way the story was reported and allows the case to be argued from several points of view. The procedures are similar to those in the previous case: individual preparation, small-group discussion, whole-class deliberation and debriefing, and several writing stages.

Sharing each group's point of view on a wikispace will prompt a deeper understanding of the case, highlight the idea of collaboration, and lessen the temptation to plagiarize. Students will need to transform the notes of others into tighter arguments and more coherent thought as they respond to the problem.

Discussing and writing about the case may help learners connect with the conflicts with authority that are featured in James Hanley's "The Butterfly," Walter Dean Myers' *Monster*, Sherman Alexie's *The Lone Ranger and Tonto Fistfight in Heaven*, Chinua Achebe's *Things Fall Apart*, George Orwell's *Animal Farm*, Aldous Huxley's *Brave New World*, and Lois Lowry's *The Giver*.

EPISODE 2.1. Hand out and discuss the case presented in Figure 4–2.

EPISODE 2.2. Have students discuss the problem in small groups, then post their position on the wikispace. The following small-group exchange (although the students stumble a bit) captures some typical responses from the point of view of the complaining homeowners.

Sylvia: All right, what are we saying?

Hugo: Basically, these kids made their own ball field and spent their own money.

Greg: Our main thing is safety. They shouldn't be allowed to keep the field.

Hugo: They found all this weird stuff in there. What happens when some little kid falls and gets cut and infection sets in and he dies?

Greg: That means they made it safer for kids. That's not going to help our position.

Freda: They could hit the ball out of the field and break a window or something and make too much noise.

Figure 4–2. A Field of Their Own (or Is It?)

They can't recall the exact moment, but sometime in the spring Tommy Dolfino and Lily Mae Angstrom had the simultaneous inspiration to transform the weed-choked lot on Camden Street in their hometown of Media, Pennsylvania, into a Wiffle ball field. The lot is at the end of a cul-de-sac and connects to a wooded area behind a row of homes in the middle-class neighborhood. The lot and the woods are owned by the town of Media; the land is protected from development because it helps to protect nearby homes from flooding.

Tommy and Lily Mae persuaded six of their friends who also love to play Wiffle ball to help them clear the lot of weeds, carve out a baseball diamond, and construct outfield walls. At first they wanted to make the field a replica of Citzens Bank Park, home field of their beloved Phillies. But Tommy, inspired by photographs of old Shibe Park, former home of both the Phillies and the Athletics, convinced the others to model their field after that park instead. They marked off the dimensions of their Wiffle ball field in smaller but exact proportion to the original Shibe Park. They collected scrap lumber from the local Woodbyrne Millworks, including slightly damaged sheets of plywood, and raised tall right and center field walls and a low wall in left field. They even painted facsimile advertisements for Butch's Market, Longines Fine Watches, and Baumann Milk.

While cleaning up the lot, they found and properly discarded three automobile tires, a shopping cart, some broken glass, and rusty paint cans. Some of the waste could have been a hazard to the environment and to children playing in the lot. They estimated that they worked a combined total of seventy-five hours and spent about sixty dollars out of their own pockets to make their dream come alive. Passersby would ask what they were doing and sometimes compliment them for their service to the community. When the field was complete, the friends seemed never to tire of playing game after game of Wiffle ball in the early evening and on weekend afternoons.

(continues)

Figure 4–2. A Field of Their Own (or Is It?) *(continued)*

After two weeks some neighbors began to complain. They didn't like the idea of having eight adolescents hanging around their street day after day. Sometimes in their enthusiasm over a great defensive play or a majestic home run, the friends would cheer and shout encouragement. They were teens playing outside and saw no need to speak in whispers. A neighbor in the house closest to the field worried that a hard-hit ball could damage the siding on his house or worse, smash through a window.

The complaining neighbors asked their councilwoman, Catherine Mooney, to ban playing Wiffle ball on the town-owned lot. She was reluctant to arrest the teenagers for trespassing, and it seemed unreasonable to prohibit them from doing something that seemed so wholesome. At the same time, she needed to honor requests from her constituents to protect them from the adolescents who were upsetting the peace and tranquility in the otherwise quiet neighborhood.

The councilwoman decided to host a neighborhood meeting at which all sides in the dispute could work toward a resolution. She proposed the following format:

1. Groups of like-minded interested parties will prepare for the meeting by studying the facts, developing their own arguments, and anticipating the arguments of others regarding the central question, *Should the town ban the eight adolescents from playing Wiffle ball on the field that they constructed?* Each group will reach a consensus about what action should be taken, and explain why.

2. During the meeting, a representative from each group will be the primary spokesperson for the group. (After all primary spokespersons have presented their group's position, other members of each team can contribute, following the procedures in step 3 below.)

3. After the first speaker has presented his or her group's position, all other speakers will begin by summarizing what the

(continues)

Figure 4–2. A Field of Their Own (or Is It?) (*continued*)

previous speaker has said and verifying the accuracy of this summary.

4. Everyone will keep track of the arguments by taking notes during the meeting.

5. After all groups have had a chance to speak and respond in this open forum, all participants, individually, will write letters to the councilwoman offering advice.

The Groups

- *Neighbors who want the teens banned from playing in the lot.* They are concerned about their safety, about peace and quiet, and about protecting their property from damage. They also worry that it will be much more difficult to sell property near a vacant lot where teenagers hang out. This could cost them money in the future. They know the town owns the property and that it is protected from development.

- *Neighbors who are sympathetic to the friends looking for a place to play Wiffle ball.* These neighbors do not live immediately adjacent to the lot. Every day they see a group of adolescents playing ball on a field they constructed themselves. They know that teens can get in trouble in many ways, but this group of adolescents seems to have channeled their energies in a positive way.

- *The teens who worked hard constructing the ball field.* They know the vacant lot was an eyesore and a hazard. No one was using it for anything constructive. Through their hard work, they have made the neighborhood better by providing a great place for them to play. They have worked very hard and have spent their own money to make the field. They feel it would be unfair to take it away from them.

- *The teens' parents.* They know their children are staying healthier by being physically active. In addition, when the

(continues)

Figure 4–2. A Field of Their Own (or Is It?) (*continued*)

teens are playing on the Wiffle ball field, they are safe and are not getting into mischief. These young people have worked hard and invested their own money to improve the neighborhood.

- *Local merchants who see an opportunity to advertise their businesses inexpensively on the outfield walls of the field.* They have supported these teenagers by supplying surplus paint and scrap lumber.

- *The officers from the Media police department.* These officers know from long experience that bored teens get in trouble during the summer. They would rather see the group of teens constructing a ball field and playing on it. They are glad that the vacant lot is cleaned up. It is never safe when you have tall weeds and debris in a vacant lot. Although they have an obligation to protect the peace and the property in the community, they hope that the neighbors will tolerate a little noise.

Put It in Writing

While Ms. Mooney found the public forum useful, she's having a hard time evaluating everything that was said and forming an overall conclusion. Write to her about your personal perspective:

- In an *introduction,* let Ms. Mooney know that you are aware of the problem facing the neighbors, the group of friends, and the city council. Summarize the case and preview the discussion that will follow.

- In a *series of paragraphs,* represent fairly the argument of each side in the dispute, whether you agree with the position or not.

- Make a recommendation for resolving the dispute. Support your argument with relevant information and explain how the information is significant.

You'll probably make several attempts at writing your letter before you are satisfied with the finished product. Be sure to get some editorial help before you submit your final version.

Sylvia: What would someone say against that?

Greg: The noise thing, we live near a park and you can hear noises from kids playing and it's no big deal.

Hugo: There are unsupervised teens in an isolated area.

Freda: And the city councilwoman has to honor the request from the neighbors to consider banning the teens.

Sylvia: Wait. We are, like, arguing against everyone else?

Greg: We are arguing that these are teenage boys who are strong enough to whack the ball really hard and break a neighbor's window.

Sylvia: So, what are our reasons?

Greg: It's not safe.

Freda: It's too loud.

Hugo: You can't stereotype the teens to assume that they are wholesome. The people who are trying to sell their homes, they don't want a gang of kids hanging around.

EPISODE 2.3. The students present the competing views of their assigned roles in a class forum, evaluating the various merits. Each class member should also have an opportunity to discuss the case from her or his own perspective, following the same deliberative procedures: acknowledge previous contributors, respectfully assess their contributions, and add your own analysis.

EPISODE 2.4. Drawing from their individual notes and the postings on the wikispace, students draft, revise, and edit their individual responses.

Summing Up

After writing the letters required in these lessons (or similar ones you design yourself), your students will have developed a degree of conscious awareness of the process. A prompt like the one that follows helps them clearly see the procedures they now command.

From their responses you'll be able to tell whether they are ready to transfer their thinking to new situations.

I know my students next year will be nervous when I ask them to write two- or three-page letters about these or similar cases. Doing so will seem impossible.

Write a letter to these future sixth graders explaining step by step how you were able to write such a highly developed letter. Consider the following questions:

- How did you approach the process?
- What class activities helped you to complete the letter?
- How helpful was the information in the assignment?
- To what extent was the discussion in your small group a help?
- To what extent did your notes help you? How did they help?
- What else in the preparation process helped you write your letter?
- What else would have helped you write your letter?

Conclude by briefly summarizing the points you've made.

What Makes This a Structured Process Approach?

As we hope we have demonstrated in this book, we believe that kids learn best when actively engaged in activities that interest them. This is the foundation of a structured process approach. Now that you have seen what teaching this way looks like, we'll lay out the basic principles that guided our planning and that might guide yours, too, going forward:

- The teacher usually identifies the task, such as writing an argumentation essay, although students may participate in deciding what they want to learn how to write. Even with the task identified, students often begin learning the processes through familiar activities such as reasoning logically or considering competing points of view.

- Learning begins with *activity* rather than with the product of that learning. For example, the instruction in Chapter 1, rather than beginning with a sample essay, begins with an activity in which students, in small groups, make judgments about a small body of information and link units of thought in a coherent and organized way.

- The teacher designs and sequences activities that allow students to move through increasingly challenging problems of the same type. In the instruction in Chapter 1, students first determine bases for their class' most popular interests, for an appropriate mascot, and for the best dog/owner matchups. In Chapter 2, they identify and evaluate opposing points of view.

- Students' learning is highly social, involving continual talk with one another as they learn procedures and strategies for particular kinds of writing. Throughout structured process instruction, students participate in whole-class and small-group discussions as they grapple with various defining problems and writing activities.

- The teacher designs the activities that take students through the particular writing process that produces the final product. However, in class, *the students are the ones talking and doing.* After helping the students identify the procedures in advancing an argument, the teacher has students apply them in increasingly complex situations. The teacher's role is primarily to help students apply the strategies, not exercise a heavy hand in leading discussions and guiding the writing.

A structured process approach therefore places the teacher in the role of designer and orchestrator of student activity through which the *students themselves* make many of the decisions about how to write and how to assess the quality of their writing. Figure 5–1 is a more comprehensive list of principles that guide this approach. We and other teachers influenced by George Hillocks have outlined this approach in a number of publications, including Hillocks 1975, 2006, 2011; Hillocks, McCabe, and McCampbell 1971; Johannessen, Kahn, and Walter 1982; Johannessen, Kahn, and Walter 2009; Kahn, Walter, and Johannessen 1984; Lee 1993; McCann, Johannessen, Kahn, Smagorinsky, and Smith 2005; Smagorinsky 2008; and Smagorinsky, McCann, and Kern 1987. Several of these titles are available for free download at www.coe .uga.edu/~smago/Books/Free_Downloadable_Books.htm.

Figure 5–1. Principles of a Structured Process Approach

1. Instruction allows students to develop procedures for how to compose in relation to particular kinds of tasks. The processes that students use to write argumentation essays, for example, are different from those used to write fictional narratives.

2. Because different tasks require different procedures, writing instruction cannot rely solely on general strategies. Rather than simply learning "prewriting" as an all-purpose strategy, students learn how to prewrite in connection with a specific genre—argument, for example, in which case small groups of students might interpret a data set or assume a number of competing points of view.

3. With writing instruction focused on specific tasks, students work toward clear and specific goals with a particular reader or community of readers in mind. For example, students might write to the manager of a local animal shelter advising her how to match potential pet owners with the animals available for adoption.

4. Even with clear and specific goals, thinking and writing are open-ended. While all students in a class might agree that shoppers want to feel safe and secure at the shopping mall, they will probably suggest a variety of ways to assure that safety.

5. Composing is a highly social act rather than the work of an individual. Students discuss their compositions with peers at every stage of development. In a structured process approach, people learn to write by *talking* as well as by writing. The oral exchanges in which students try out their arguments and evaluate the arguments of others are rehearsals and opportunities to generate ideas for their written arguments.

(continues)

Figure 5–1. Principles of a Structured Process Approach (*continued*)

6. The teacher identifies the criteria used to assess the writing. Students often help develop these evaluative criteria by discussing what they value in the writing they read. When the writing is tied to large-scale assessment, such as writing a persuasive argument for a district or state exam, the criteria might already be in place.

7. The teacher *scaffolds* students' learning of procedures by designing activities and providing materials that the students may manipulate. Instruction begins with simple, manageable aspects. For example, instruction in how to write arguments begins with activities in which students explore reasoning logically and choosing one potential school mascot over another. Instruction then progresses through more challenging aspects of the writing, such as anticipating and evaluating competing points of view. Attention to form comes later in the instruction when students have developed content to write about, rather than earlier, as is often the case with instruction in how to write the five-paragraph theme.

8. When possible, the teacher provides additional readerships for students' writing, such as having the students post their writing in the classroom or on a classroom wikispace or submit their writing to a contest, the school newspaper, the school literary magazine, and so on.

Designing Structured Process Instruction

A structured process approach to teaching writing involves two key ideas: *environmental teaching* and *inquiry instruction* (Hillocks 1995).

Environmental Teaching

One important assumption that underlies environmental teaching is the belief that *each task we ask students to do involves unique ways of thinking*. By way of example, think of what is involved in three types of writing tasks: defining the concept of justice, writing a fictional narrative that depicts an incidence of injustice, or composing an argument for a just resolution to a problem. Each involves a consideration of the concept of justice, yet each relies on different ways of thinking and communicating one's thinking in writing. An environmental approach, then, stresses learning particular sets of *procedures* for engaging in specific sorts of *tasks*.

To help students learn to accomplish a new task, a teacher needs to involve students directly in developing strategies for undertaking that task. In other words, the teacher introduces activities that will help students learn *how* to do this new kind of thinking and writing.

A task in this sense involves both *doing* something and *thinking about how it's done* so that it can be done again with different materials. A task, then, may comprise writing a fictional narrative, or comparing and contrasting similar yet different things, defining an abstract concept such as *progress* or *success*, or arguing in favor of a solution, such as whether a group of teens should be allowed to maintain their Wiffle ball field. Our goal for students is that when they complete this task, they are able to repeat the process more independently the next time.

Inquiry Instruction

Inquiry is the particular structure through which students work, often in collaboration with one another.

Again, the teacher plays a strong role designing activities that provide the basis for students' inquiries into the problems they investigate. For writing arguments, the problem may be how to analyze information and draw conclusions, interpret evidence for a skeptical audience, or evaluate the merits of opposing positions.

The students play with materials related to the questions they hope to settle through their writing. *Play* in this sense refers to experimenting with ideas. For example, students study evidence related to proposed mascots or a dognapping neighbor. In small-group discussions, students bounce ideas off one another:

> "I think she should be put away for ten years for taking the dog."

"That's an extreme punishment for taking the dog. She thought she was saving the dog from abuse."

"But there is no evidence of abuse, just her claims. I think she just wanted to keep the dog herself."

"It was obstruction of justice, because she lied to the police, and she filed a false report. That's pretty serious but doesn't deserve a ten-year sentence."

"But it was like stealing a member of the family."

"It's different, though. There is a difference between taking a dog and taking a kid."

Students' work is open-ended in that the activities may have a number of plausible solutions or outcomes. The students arrive at different conclusions, challenge one another, persuade one another to support one position or another, and account for exceptions. As the process advances, students take into account how they will respond to reasonable opposition. Small-group discussions allow students to play with these ideas and try out solutions that may or may not ultimately figure into the final form their work takes.

What Can You Expect When Teaching Writing with This Approach?

Preparing students to write well-developed, thoughtful argumentation essays is time-consuming. The detailed, systematic sequences in this book guide students through both thinking about and writing arguments. The activities cannot attend to *all* the considerations in completing a task as complicated and interactive as writing. Realistically, before students are able to apply specific skills and strategies to new situations, they will need several experiences and appropriate feedback from you, from other students, and if possible from other readers. However, with continual reinforcement, the procedures that students generate should enable them to write persuasive arguments on future occasions when they choose or are called upon to create them.

Where Do You Go from Here?

This book and the others in this series provide specific plans you can adapt to your own teaching; they also introduce you to a process you can use to design original instruction based on your classroom and your students' needs. The guide below will help you design writing instruction using a structured process approach:

1. *Identify the task that will form the basis for your instruction.* Assuming that any general process such as "prewriting" differs depending on the demands of particular writing tasks, identify the task that will form the basis of the instruction. This task might be specified by a formal writing requirement and assessment provided by a mandate from the school, district, or state (e.g., argumentation); it might be writing that you believe is essential to your students' education (e.g., writing research reports); it might be writing that students identify as something they want to learn how to do (e.g., writing college application essays); or it might come from some other source or inspiration.

2. *Conduct an inventory of students' present writing qualities and needs.* With the task identified, you will probably want to see what students' writing of this sort looks like prior to instruction. Doing so allows you to focus on students' needs and avoid teaching strategies they already know. You could take this inventory by providing a prompt, like *Write a paragraph persuading your parents that you are old enough to stay home alone while they go to a movie.* Then assess their abilities in relation to your *task analysis* (see below).

3. *Conduct a task analysis.* Either by consulting existing sources or by going through the processes involved in carrying out the writing task yourself, identify what students need to know in order to write effectively according to the demands of readers. The task analysis should treat both *form* and *procedure.* The task analysis will also help you identify the evaluative criteria that you ultimately use to assess student work.

4. *Conduct an activity analysis.* Decide the types of activities that will engage students with materials that are likely to foster their understanding of the processes involved in the task. Identify familiar and accessible materials (e.g., favorite activities and school mascots) for the early stages of their learning, and more complex materials (e.g., competing points of view, questions of personal responsibility or bias) for subsequent activities.

5. *Design and sequence students' learning experiences so that they provide a scaffold.* Design increasingly challenging tasks of the same sort using increasingly complex materials. Sequence these activities so that students are always reiterating the process but doing so in the face of greater challenges. The activities should present continual opportunities for students to talk with one another as they learn the processes involved in carrying out the task.

6. *Consider opportunities to teach language usage in the context of learning procedures for task-related writing.* Specific kinds of writing often benefit from particular language strategies. Targeting language instruction to specific instances of its use helps overcome the problem inherent in discrete grammar instruction, which is that it fails to improve students' understanding of how to speak and write clearly.

7. *Relying on the task analysis, develop rubrics through which students clearly understand the expectations for their writing.* These rubrics may be developed in consultation with students, adopted from established criteria such as those provided for state writing tests or advanced placement exams, adopted from model rubrics available on the Internet, created by examining a set of student work that represents a range of performance, and so on.

8. *Provide many opportunities during the learning process for feedback and revision.* Students should be given many occasions to get feedback on drafts of their writing. This feedback can come by way of peer response groups, your written

response to their writing, writing conferences with you, or other means of response.

A Structured Process Approach and Professional Learning Communities

Currently, many school faculties constitute a professional learning community made up of collaborative teams. Structured process instruction is particularly effective in this context. Teachers together develop instruction and analyze student work. Teams use the student writing produced during the instructional sequence as a basis for discussing what worked, what students are struggling with, and what should be done differently or what needs to be added to the instruction. The teams collaboratively design rubrics for scoring student work so that expectations for students are consistent. Collecting data on student performance from pretest to final product allows the group to evaluate student growth, reflect on the strengths and weaknesses of the instruction, and plan future classroom activities.

Our own teaching has shown us that this approach can greatly improve students' writing. We look forward to hearing how you have adapted this approach to your own teaching and helped your students learn how to use written expression to meet their responsibilities as students, writers, friends, communicators, and citizens.

Questions for Reflection

1. What place does writing argumentation essays have in the middle school and high school curriculum?

2. Argumentation depends on logical reasoning. To what extent is it possible to teach students how to reason logically?

3. Describe the process a writer would follow in producing an argument. How is the process different from that of writing a story or a research report?

4. Writing a persuasive argument relies on the ability to imagine and evaluate competing points of view. How can you help your students refine this skill?

5. What challenges might younger writers encounter with conventions and mechanics as they attempt to write an argument? How can you teach the key concepts proactively?

6. It can be hard to agree what elements define good argumentation writing, especially because many of the writers we admire break with convention. How can you help students define for themselves what distinguishes a well-written argument?

7. How would you link argumentation writing with literature featuring themes of personal responsibility, justice, competing points of view? What are the advantages of doing so?

8. How can visual images or other appeals to the senses help students plan and produce argumentation essays?

References

Applebome, Peter. 2008. "Build a Wiffle Ball Field and Lawyers Will Come." *New York Times*, July 10.

Blumenthal, Ralph. 2008. "Tale of Dead Texas Dog Bites Mayor Who Told It." *New York Times*, February 13.

Crowhurst, M. 1988. *Research Review: Patterns of Development in Writing Persuasive Argumentative Discourse.* University of British Columbia. ERIC Document 299596. Accessed online January 5, 2011.

———. 1990. "Teaching and Learning the Writing of Persuasive/ Argumentative Discourse." *Canadian Journal of Education* 15 (Autumn): 348–59.

Graff, G. 2003. *Clueless in Academe: How Schooling Obscures the Life of the Mind.* New Haven: Yale University Press.

Hillocks, G. 1975. *Observing and Writing.* Urbana, IL: National Council of Teachers of English.

———. 1986. *Research on Written Composition: New Directions for Teaching.* Urbana, IL: National Conference on Research in English and Educational Resources Information Center.

———. 1995. *Teaching Writing as Reflective Practice.* New York: Teachers College Press.

———. 2002. *The Testing Trap: How State Writing Assessments Control Learning.* New York: Teachers College Press.

———. 2005. "The Focus on Form vs. Content in Teaching Writing." *Research in the Teaching of English* 40: 238–48.

———. 2006. *Narrative Writing: Learning a New Model for Teaching.* Portsmouth, NH: Heinemann.

———. 2010. "Teaching Argument for Critical Thinking and Writing: An Introduction." *English Journal* 99 (6): 24–32.

———. 2011. *Teaching Argument Writing, Grades 6–12: Supporting Claims with Relevant Evidence and Clear Reasoning.* Portsmouth, NH: Heinemann.

Hillocks, G., E. Kahn, and L. Johannessen. 1983. "Teaching Defining Strategies as a Mode of Inquiry." *Research in the Teaching of English* 17: 275–84.

Hillocks, G., B. McCabe, and J. McCampbell. 1971. *The Dynamics of English Instruction, Grades 7–12.* New York: Random House. Retrieved August 4, 2006, from www.coe.uga.edu/~smago /Books/Dynamics/Dynamics_home.htm.

Hillocks, G., and J. F. McCampbell. 1965. *Talks on the Teaching of English.* Euclid, OH: Project English Demonstration Center and Case Western Reserve University.

Johannessen, L. R., E. Kahn, and C. C. Walter. 1982. *Designing and Sequencing Pre-writing Activities.* Urbana, IL: National Council of Teachers of English. Retrieved July 2, 2008 from www.coe.uga .edu/~smago/Books/Designing_and_Sequencing.pdf.

———. 2009. *Writing About Literature,* 2d ed. revised and updated. Urbana, IL: National Council of Teachers of English.

Johnson, T. S., P. Smagorinsky, L. Thompson, and P. G. Fry. 2003. "Learning to Teach the Five-Paragraph Theme." *Research in the Teaching of English* 38 (November): 136–76.

Kahn, E., C. Walter, and L. Johannessen. 1984. *Writing About Literature.* Urbana, IL: National Council of Teachers of English.

Karbach, J. 1987. "Using Toulmin's Model of Argumentation." *Journal of Writing* 6 (1): 81–91.

Kneupper, C. W. 1978. "Teaching Argument: An Introduction to the Toulmin Model." *College Composition and Communication* 29 (3): 237–41.

Lee, C. D. 1993. *Signifying as a Scaffold for Literary Interpretation: The Pedagogical Implications of an African American Discourse Genre.* Urbana, IL: National Council of Teachers of English.

Marshall, J., and J. Smith. 1997. "Teaching as We're Taught: The University's Role in the Education of English Teachers." *English Education* 29: 246–68.

McCann, T. M. 1989. "Student Argumentative Writing Knowledge and Ability at Three Grade Levels." *Research in the Teaching of English* 23 (1): 62–76.